THE 12 GATES OF HEAVEN

DISCOVER YOUR GOD GIVEN POTENTIAL
AND
AWAKEN TO YOUR LIFE PURPOSE

JUDY FAASS

The 12 Gates of Heaven: Discover Your God Given Potential and Awaken to Your Life Purpose
ISBN: 978-0-578-68860-2
Library of Congress Control Number: 2020907792

Unless otherwise noted, all Scripture quotations are from the New Kings James version of the Bible in the public domain.

Photo credit: Brown Bear Cover Image - National Park Service - Kevyn Jalone
Photo credit: Buffalo at Yellowstone Cover Image - BorisFromStockdale at the English language Wikipedia
Drawing credit: Jacob's Ladder Coloring Page - A. Skib - CC BY-NC 4.0 License
All other photos, drawings, figures, tables and images are property of the author or are public domain.

Book design by Judy Faass and Freedom Spirit Prison Outreach
FreedomSpiritPrisonOutreach@gmail.com
www.facebook.com/PrisonAdvocacy

Printed in the United States of America

All spiritual growth, 100% of it, is about releasing or eliminating rather than attaining something, because we are already IT spiritually.

~ Michael B Beckwith

Time is life. Therefore, waste your time and waste your life, or master your time and master your life!

~ Alan Lakein

Whether you think you can, or you think you can't – you're right.

~ Henry Ford

Whether your path has been smooth or rocky, your life gentle or traumatic, of this you may be certain: you are among the most courageous souls in the Universe. Were that not true, you would not be here now.

~ Robert Schwartz

Dedication

To God, my Creator. Thank you for all of my many blessings and for supporting my decision to come to earth as a courageous spirit. Thank you for loving me, thank you for teaching me about abundance, love, peace, and forgiveness, and thank you for teaching me the Truth through your Word.

To my beautiful Angel and friend, Lehahiah (34) who has taught me divine obedience, discipline, loyalty and devotion while keeping me connected to the supernatural and the spirit world. You strongly encouraged me to write this book. Thank you for always being there, and thank you for not giving up on me!

To everyone on the 'inside' and on the 'outside' of prison walls, who have supported my desire to change hearts and transform lives through the Freedom Spirit Prison Outreach.

To everyone who wants to break free from the mundane and actively pursue their life purpose - this book is for all of you!

- Judy Faass

Contents

The Mental Gates of the North

Appendix

Figures and Tables

Introduction

A very long time ago, as a young Native American boy, I often played and ran through the pastures on the land belonging to my tribe. While running, one particular day, I saw an eagle in the sky that seemed to be calling to me…. "follow me"…. so I did. He led me to a beautiful river bank and when I stopped running, I saw a beautiful mountain in front of me. I was facing east, and the sun was rising up from behind the mountain, yet the sun didn't quite show itself fully; instead, a bright light emanated and flowed across the upper mountain ridge. I said, "who are YOU, are you my Creator?" The bright light responded, "I AM who I AM". A bit puzzled, I responded, "then who am I?" The bright light said, "YOU are who I made you to be, but you know not, and you are not yet ready." The light continued, "In a little while we will meet again, and you will see."

As it came to pass, I would not live long enough to finish my earthly journey. I died at 19 years of age; at that exact same spot on that river bank. I was hit in the head with the butt end of a rifle and killed by soldiers, ironically during 'warrior training'; but nevertheless, I was sent home. Upon returning home, I felt incomplete, so I asked to come back, I was eager to finish my earthly journey, and to learn my life lessons.

Eventually I returned, and here I am once again, this time incarnating as a female. I write this book, many years later in this new lifetime. I'm living life to the fullest, and enjoying every moment! And yes, after many years in this life, I made it back to my mountainous home and my beautiful river, flowing with the richness of life. I am now fully awakened and living my spiritual life purpose in the beautiful mountains of Colorado.

Early in this new lifetime, I found my path along my journey and I have traveled through many gates to get to this point. Therefore, it is with great respect to my Creator, my angels and my guides, that I humbly bring to you this journey… this thing called life. Come with me as we travel through… *The 12 Gates of Heaven.*

Let's begin.

Do You Know Who You Are?

God, our Creator, will find us - even if we choose to walk away. We are important to Him; He created us and allowed our spirit to come to earth, to experience a human existence, so that we would be able to fulfill our purpose and to further learn the lessons of life. You are a favored, protected and blessed child of God. But as a human, you also have free will. So, if you choose to depart and walk away, God will let you. He will call to you, but if you are living in the flesh, living in the natural, unable to see or hear from the Divine, then you will continue to live separated from Him, following others, like sheep to the slaughter until you come to a point where you answer the call. Remember the scripture about the narrow gate? What do you think that means.... the narrow gate?

"Enter through the narrow gate; for the gate is wide and the way is broad that leads to destruction, and there are many who enter through it. For the gate is small and the way is narrow that leads to life, and there are few who find it." **(Matthew 7:13-14)** The narrow gate leads to life. So, choose life. Right?

Many people talk about God, their faith, and their beliefs, but they actually are far from living the life that was designed for them. They don't really have a personal relationship with their Creator, and they honestly don't know who they are.

God is patient, He will wait for you, as time does not exist in the spirit realm, only here on earth. You can choose to live in the natural or live in the supernatural from which you came. It is written that he knows the plans that he has for you, plans to give you a hope and a future and an expected end. It is written that you will call upon God, and pray to Him and He will listen to you. You will seek Him and find Him when you search with all of your heart. Once you find God, He will bring you back from your captivity. **(Jeremiah 29:11-14)** When you can see and hear, it's up to you how your respond to your supernatural calling. You can obey and turn to God, or you can continue on your own path. It's your choice; but you know the saying as well as I do – "If you want to make God laugh, tell Him what YOUR plans are". Funny, right? But you know it is true. It is also written that if you delight in the Lord, He will give you the desires of your heart. **(Psalm 37:4)** That scripture doesn't mean that God will shower you with large houses, fancy cars, and other coveted material possessions that YOU want, it means that when you operate in the spirit, from the heart, not the flesh, you will clearly see the life and purpose that your Heavenly Father has prepared for you. It is written that we are his workmanship, created in Christ Jesus for good works, which God prepared beforehand so that we would walk in them. **(Ephesians 2:10)** So, you see? He has already prepared the works that you will do and he is just waiting for you to awaken to YOUR true purpose and YOUR life path. Are you ready?

God is with you wherever you are, whether you see it or sense it or not. You have a "direct connect" to God. You just have to plug in; He is waiting. It is written that He will not leave you nor forsake you! **(Deuteronomy 31:6)** This point, that God is always with you and won't forsake you, is such a strong point that it is mentioned two other times in the bible! **(1 Chronicles 28:20 and Hebrews 13:5-6)** And, if you are hung up on the word "forsake', it means that God will never abandon you, He will never renounce or give up on you! How blessed are you? To have God right by your side at all times? Receive that! Give thanks for that! He cares about you and loves you with Divine Love; the greatest of love! He created you with a purpose, and he wants you to experience abundance and success!

God will not chase you, He will wait. Your choice to accept what He has for you, is yours to make. Many people are separated from God and they move through life day after day with a Godless existence. Many wait for a tragedy to hit them, and then they cry out to God for help, or even get angry with Him for "causing" the hardship. But, why wait for a tragedy, illness or a hardship to take you down? A life of blessings, provision, favor and abundance is waiting for you now, but in order to accept it and live a Godly life, you have to know WHO you are first. You are a blessed child of God! Give that some thought. Your current circumstances may not be telling you that, but that is because you are living in the natural, you need to step outside of your "body" step away from the flesh and the ego, and live from your spirit. Step into the supernatural! God doesn't look at your body, he looks at your spirit. It is written that God is Spirit and those who worship Him must worship Him in Spirit and in Truth. **(John 4:24)**

To further tell you about who you are, have you ever noticed the scripture in **(Genesis 1:26-28)**, the very FIRST book of the bible? It is written that God said "Let US make man in OUR image, according to OUR likeness." Have you ever wondered why He speaks in the plural? 'US' refers to God, Jesus, and the Holy Spirit. Remember that

Jesus was Spirit also, before he came to earth as a human. So, this scripture is telling you that YOU were originally created as Spirit! You were originally created in the likeness of God, Jesus and the Holy Spirit (the entire Trinity)! So that is how the trinity sees you! As Spirit! You are a manifestation of the most high God and you were created in His image! You are currently having a human experience, because you were strong and courageous and decided to come to earth. I call it Earth School, because if you think about it, we sure do learn a lot here through life challenges and life lessons. If you study the works of Robert Schwartz (*Your Soul's Plan* and *Your Soul's Gift*) you will come to realize that you even planned this trip to earth before you were born. It's fascinating! Study and understand who you are and why you are here!

When we take on this human experience, from spirit, the first thing that happens to us is that we forget who we are! Your experience is designed that way on purpose! Think about that! Why would you come here with all of the answers? In that way, there would be no learning to do. You must seek, you must find, you must discover, you must learn! Once you become awakened to who you are, you will be amazed what you are able to attract and what is able to come your way! Life becomes more exciting, more adventurous and your past will make more sense to you! You see, nothing happens without purpose; I challenge you to meditate, sit quietly and give yourself a life review. Go back as far as you can remember and think of everything that has happened to you or that you have experienced thus far since you were born here on earth. Try to understand the WHY behind those experiences and try to figure out the lesson that you learned by going through them! You will come to find that most of your experiences were planned and you were supposed to go through them. You will also discover that you did not go through these experiences alone; God, your guides, and your angels were right there with you all along!

When I did this exercise, I began to remember things that happened to me as a small child. Prompted by my guides, "remember that?" Yes I would say.... My mother told me that I was "lucky" or that my experience was coincidence... "Nope", they said. "That was US. We brought you through that!" Wow! I kept going, remembering my experiences.... one by one....while my guides kept giving me the same answer until I got it! I finally came to the realization that I had been carried and protected all along! I had no idea! That session ended with tears streaming down my face. After completing this exercise, I began to experience my true awakening and began to realize who I truly was. It was amazing and I hope you get the same result when you take the time to go through the same exercise!

You see, God is no respecter of persons **(Acts 10:34)**. He will come along side you just like anyone else. He sees you as his creation and he sees you as spirit. Once you awaken to the truth, and you believe with your heart that you ARE a blessed child of god, a spirit having a human experience, then all things will begin to make sense and you will be lead on a path of freedom and victory! Start a personal relationship with your Creator now. Ask Him to show you who you are! Trust me, He will; but get ready for the ride! It's amazing! It is written that we as humans make the Word of God of no effect through our own traditions **(Mark 7:13)**. So why choose to live in the flesh? Why choose to live in the world? Why choose to live in the natural? Why choose to exist like sheep going to slaughter? Break away from the herd! Start living in the supernatural! Start living by following the purpose and path that was set before you! Start living with abundant blessings! Change your normal, and awaken to the 'spirit' you!

You have power! And, this isn't any ordinary power that you have inside you, it's the SAME power that raised Christ from the dead! **(Ephesians 1:19-20)** Go ahead! Read about it! Receive it! Celebrate that! BE that! Awaken to who you are!

Let me remind you of a story that you know, but may have forgotten about: Jacob's Ladder. In **(Genesis 28: 11-17)**, it is written about how Jacob found out who <u>he</u> was. Pay attention to what happened to him when he "walked away" from his family, his deceptive and manipulative life; he had an amazing encounter with God through a dream! You can do the same!

Jacob's Dream

He [Jacob] came to a certain place and spent the night there, because the sun had set; and he took one of the stones of the place and put it under his head, and lay down in that place. He had a dream, and behold, a ladder was set on the earth with its top reaching to heaven; and behold, the angels of God were ascending

10

and descending on it. And behold, the Lord stood above it and said, "I am the Lord, the God of your father Abraham and the God of Isaac; the land on which you lie, I will give it to you and to your descendants. Your descendants will also be like the dust of the earth, and you will spread out to the west and to the east and to the north and to the south; and in you and in your descendants shall all the families of the earth be blessed. Behold, I am with you and will keep you wherever you go, and will bring you back to this land; for I will not leave you until I have done what I have promised you." Then Jacob awoke from his sleep and said, "Surely the Lord is in this place, and I did not know it." He was afraid and said, "I am in awe of this place! This is none other than the house of God, and this is the GATE of heaven." **(Genesis 28: 11-17)**

The Hebrew word for GATE is Shaar which translates door, entrance, or an opening. So, Jacob was recognizing the "place" where he was as being an entrance or an opening to the house of God, through this gate, door or portal which he was shown. He discovered that this gate is where man has access to heaven, where prayers are heard and delivered to the heavens, where God's provision and abundance is handed down. You probably have heard the saying "As above, so below"? This refers to the same concept, that we CAN experience heaven while here on earth! Similarly, a familiar passage of scripture to you may be the Lord's Prayer where it is written – Our Father, who art in heaven, hallowed be thy Name. Thy Kingdom come. Thy will be done ON EARTH AS IT IS IN HEAVEN… See? You have known this concept all along, you may just not have been aware of its impact on your life. Jacob got to experience this truth in a life changing dream. God speaks to us through various means; you just have to find the best "direct connect" for you! Dreams? Meditation? Prayer? God is listening, you only need to speak and ASK for His help and He will show you the truth!

You will find, later in the bible, that the MAIN GATE is actually Jesus. You will read this in (John 1:51) where it is written, "Truly truly I say to all of you, you will see the heavens open and the angels of God ascending and descending on the Son of Man." The ascending and descending of angels, as mentioned in Jacob's dream (Genesis 28:12), is a symbolic representation of the uninterrupted and active living communication that existed between Jesus and God the Father. In his dream, Jacob was discovering this living communication first hand and it was "in this place" that he realized that this communication was something that God wanted to share with him as well. He had discovered the Gate of Heaven! When Jesus came to earth, he set aside his Glory to become a human being. Likewise, you set aside the knowledge of your spirit when YOU became a human being. Don't you think if Jesus needed this communication with God involving the ascending and descending of angels, how much more YOU need the same? Believe and receive this concept!

God desires to have a relationship with the "spirit you". He desires to make you aware of His presence, to give you spiritual perspective and to do His work through your life. God wants you to encounter Him, just like Jacob did; to trust Him and to walk your own personal journey with Him. God is very interested in making clear to us WHO we are, ahead of the priority of WHAT He wants us to do. He realizes you dwell in a human body (also known as a dwelling and tent in the bible). But in order for you to maintain this spiritual connection between you and God, you must first become awakened to who you are! You need to acknowledge that you have access to this ladder, this stairway to heaven as it's often called, this spiritual highway where messages travel up and down between heaven and earth. The angels are messengers; your prayers and communications are carried "up" to the heavens, and communications and instructions travel back "down" to you on earth. I like to call these "downloads" from God. I think that before I became awakened, these communications used to come down in the form of a Divine 2x4 upside my head! But now, I'm more plugged in, I know who I am, and I listen to and look forward to the downloads as they come! And believe me, once you are awakened to who you are, the downloads come fast and often! Your angels are standing by to help you, all you have to do is ASK them for help. Keep your angels employed, they are there to travel this spiritual highway and to help you with your spiritual journey through the gates!

It is written in **(Ephesians 2:19-22)** So then you are no longer strangers and aliens, but you are fellow citizens with the saints, and are of God's household, having been built on the foundation of the apostles and prophets, Christ Jesus Himself being the corner stone, in whom the whole building, being fitted together, is growing into a holy temple in the Lord, in whom you also are being built together into a dwelling of God in the Spirit.

As we discovered in **(Genesis 1)**, you were created in the likeness and image of God the Father, Jesus, and the Holy Spirit. According to the Ephesians scripture that we just read, you are "One" with the Divine.

Now that you have a better handle on your spiritual identity, I would like to introduce you to the 12 gates of heaven. Think of these gates as life challenges and life experiences that have been placed in your path during your lifetime, in order to help you develop certain qualities needed for your life purpose and your life plan. When you unlock these gates, and do the work to travel through them, you will discover your God given potential and awaken to your life purpose.

Always keep in mind that Jesus is the MAIN gate; think of these 12 gates as a needed accessory to your mission; an accessory that will help you to enhance, enrich and further your new or existing relationship with your Creator.

Do you NOW know who you are? Are you ready?

Let's dive in!

Traveling Through the 12 Gates

Discovering Your Purpose and Your Life Path

by

Understanding Life Lessons and Challenges

Mental Gates of the North

Spiritual Gates of the East

Physical Gates of the West

Emotional Gates of the South

The 12 gates are openings or gateways through which you travel. Communications are able to ASCEND FROM you and DESCEND TO you from the spiritual realms and the heavens. The gates give us the opportunity to discover, explore and learn life lessons. They present challenges and an opportunity to "do the work"; the end result being the discovery of your life purpose and your life plan. We "travel through" the gates; we do not "pass" through them in one direction. When we do the work, we often move in a forward direction with our life, but we often backslide as well. So we often have to travel through the same gate multiple times in order to get it right. We do not simply unlock a gate and 'pass" through it. We travel through it, coming and going, ascending and descending, back and forth, until our life lesson is learned.

So what do the cardinal directions of north, south, east, and west have to do with any of this? I'm glad you asked! These directions are mentioned throughout the bible and you just read about them in Jacob's Dream, remember?

> "Your descendants will also be like the dust of the earth, and you will spread out to the west and to the east and to the north and to the south; and in you and in your descendants shall all the families of the earth be blessed." **(Genesis 28:14)**.

(Psalm 107:1-3) also explains this rather well. Have a look:

Give thanks to the LORD, for He is good;

His loving devotion endures forever.

Let the redeemed of the LORD say so,

whom He has redeemed from the hand of the enemy

and gathered from the lands,

from east and west, from north and south.

This particular psalm states that the redeemed will enter the house of God after being gathered from ALL directions. Doesn't it make sense then, that there would therefore be gateways of Divine communication from all directions? Of course it does!

Read on to discover more bible scriptures that mention these cardinal directions, have a look!

(Luke 13:29) And they will come from east and west and from north and south, and will recline at the table in the Kingdom of God.

(Genesis 13:14) The LORD said to Abram, after Lot had separated from him, "Now lift up your eyes and look from the place where you are, northward and southward and eastward and westward."

(1 Chronicles 9:24) The gatekeepers were on the four sides, to the east, west, north and south.

(Isaiah 43:5-6) Do not fear, for I am with you; I will bring your offspring from the east, and gather you from the west. I will say to the north, 'Give them up!' And to the south, 'Do not hold them back'. Bring My sons from afar and My daughters from the ends of the earth.

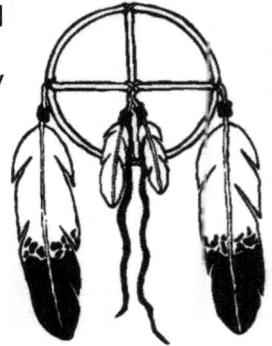

The Medicine Wheel

The medicine wheel is thought to have different meanings among different people and native tribes; it is thought to show the path to healing, health, and balance. The medicine wheel is circular, symbolizing all things are related and represents our flow of energy when we balance the Mental, Spiritual, Emotional and Physical aspects of our lives.

In addition to being a symbol of the natural cycles of life, the medicine wheel can also represent the four directions. It is said that once you realize that you are separate and removed from the earth, you become more in-tune with nature, the seasons, and thus the directions that represent them! For example...

THE EAST represents the season of Spring and may be represented by the Eagle. East is the direction that represents the gates of conception, birth and activation of new ideas, new beginnings, dreams and new ways of being that you are hoping to bring forth, like obedience. The East represents the gifts of the Spirit, visions, illumination, courage and new spiritual growth. We discover and release our spiritual power in the East, as we awaken to Spirit.

THE SOUTH represents the season of Summer and may be represented by the Wolf. South is the direction that represents the gates of youth, growth and amplification. It is a place of cultivation and nurturing, a place to grow relationships through love. The South encompasses lessons of faith, trust and humility; it represents a time for teaching and encouragement. In the South, we learn about our emotions, how to replace negativity with positivity and how to overcome fear with love.

THE WEST represents the season of Autumn and may be represented by the Bear. West is the direction that represents the gates of harvest and rest, experimentation and "testing". The West is a place where we go within ourselves to dream, harvest our intuition and integrate what we are learning. In the West, we learn about strength from adversity, renewal, balance, and transformation to a new life of servitude and gratitude. The West represents an energy of adulthood, introspection, completion, release, letting go, change and surrender.

THE NORTH represents the season of Winter and may be represented by the Buffalo. North is the direction that represents the gates of maturity and transition back to spirit. This is the place where you use your intellect to give back or reflect and share your wisdom with others. The North is also known as a place of healing and the renewing of our mind, a place of purification and transition. The North is where our ancestors await us with blessings and where they help us to 'let go' while we enter into new possibilities.

So now that we have introduced the cardinal directions of North, South, East and West, their associated seasons, and traveling through the gates, are you ready to learn more and unlock the 12 gates individually?

I am! Let's go!

The Spiritual Gates of the East

Gate #1 - Surrendering To Obedience

- Living Outside the Natural -

Gate #2 - Courageously Releasing Your Power

- Expecting Favor & Blessings -

Gate #3 - Awakening to Spirit

- Reclaiming the Knowledge of Who You Are -

Surrendering To Obedience

- Living Outside the Natural -

Let's start with first understanding a definition of "obedience", because this word can often cause strife and control issues with people. In simple terms, obedience is defined as compliance with an order, request, law or submission to another's authority. So, why should we surrender to obedience? Because being disobedient has consequences for us that, quite frankly, we really don't have time for. Life is short!

We all know right from wrong, so when we know what we SHOULD be doing (right), and we instead knowingly head down a different path (wrong), then we are being disobedient. **(James 4:17)** All things come to us from our Creator, who loves us. When we don't take care of those things, be it a job, a car, a plant, etc. we are being disobedient. When we have a gut feel as to what our future SHOULD be, but we instead knowingly choose a different path for ourselves (free will) or settle for something less, then we are being disobedient!

The good news is that God loves us in spite of our disobedience and He will still use you in spite of who you are. Remember the story of Adam and Eve? They were certainly disobedient when they chose to eat the fruit from the Tree of Good and Evil. But God didn't kick them out of the garden because of this disobedience alone; he kicked them out of the garden because they might now eat from the Tree of Life and live in this state of sin and disobedience forever! **(Genesis 3:22-24)** God kicked them out of the garden because he loved them in spite of their disobedience! Understand?

God will also use the weak to do His work, so that no man may boast. **(1 Corin 1:27-29)** Remember how he used Moses? As a leader? Who had to be strong and courageous to lead the Israelites out of Egypt even though, by his own admission, he was "slow of speech", and not the best speaker in the world? Moses didn't really feel like a credible leader who spoke with conviction, yet God used him anyway! God encouraged Moses and taught him how to obey and how to lead

His people out of Egypt. God further asked Moses "what is in your hand" to make him see and understand that he had "God's power" all along, he just needed to recognize it and use it. If you don't remember that story in the bible, go back and read it **(Exodus 4)**. It's a very powerful story!

So, I have to ask you, what is in YOUR hand? What has God given you that you are not using 100% in YOUR life? What has God given you that you have chosen to ignore (disobedience) and what has God asked you to do, that you know you SHOULD do, but you don't because you don't have the faith or confidence in yourself to complete the task as you should? I'll give you a minute to think about that. Take a break from reading and really give this some deep thought. Write it down and reflect on it if you have to. Your answers will be essential to traveling through this gate.

~

OK, are you back? Did you give that some serious consideration? Because if you don't get that exercise, it will be very difficult for you to walk in obedience and to find the strength and power that you already have inside of you. It's very important that you do the work and that you step OUT of the natural and INTO the supernatural. You have to step out in faith. What is that in your hand (Moses)? Is it simply a sheep herding rod? A Staff? Or, is it the Rod of God or the Staff of God that has the power to part the Red Sea in order to save the people that you have been instructed to "lead"? How about you? Did you get that figured out for yourself? What is in YOUR hand?

When God tells you to do something or tells you to move to a certain location, or take a certain job, or volunteer for something within your community, He is doing that to give you a chance to show your obedience! It is written that God will send your provision to you "there" not here. **(1 Kings 17:2-4)** Just ask Elijah! Elijah's provision wasn't where he was; it was where God told him to go! God will do the same for you! This concept is clearly seen in the game of football – when the quarter back drops back to throw the ball to his receiver, he doesn't throw the ball right to him, now does he? NO! He throws the ball to where the receiver is "going to be"! The quarter back throws the ball "there", and the receiver catches it. God does the same thing for you! He sends your provision "there" and asks that you obey and go "there" to receive it. If God drops back and throws you a pass, you had better be "there" to catch it!

Another good example of obedience and disobedience can be seen in the Parable of the Talents **(Matt 25:14-30)** The point being made in verse 29: "For to everyone who has, more shall be given, and he will have an abundance; but from the one who does not have, even what he does have shall be taken away". In other words, if you do well with the little you have, you will be given more. I see people all the time who are begging God for a new car, a new job, or a new place to live – but, they aren't taking care of the one they have already been given! It isn't clear to them that if they don't take care of what they HAVE, they won't be given more. Its not that God is stingy and He doesn't want you to have nice things, He wants you to be obedient and take care of the "little" things that He has already given to you! Once you show obedience in this regard, you will be given more! Get out of the natural, and live in the supernatural with God! Be obedient!

God knows the plans that he has for you; to give you a hope and a future! **(Jer 29:11)** But in order for you to receive what He has for you, you must be obedient. Sure, you can try it the "other" way, I know I did! But let me cut to the chase and tell you that living in the supernatural and doing things God's way is a WHOLE lot easier AND much more rewarding! You have heard of the "school of hard knocks"? That is not God's best. God's best is walking in obedience, hearing what He wants for you and getting it done in the faith and strength that He has given to you!

How do you spend your time? Are you wasting it? Life is short! Meditate on the Word day and night **(Joshua 1:8)** Live outside the natural, and pay attention to what God has for you. These signs come through your thoughts, your visions and your dreams. Get plugged in! It takes practice to discern these "downloads" as I like to call them. But once you get the hang of it, you will become fully aware of what obedience looks like, and you will see your life take a turn for the better! God believes in abundance! He believes in your success and He knows better than you do about your life purpose here on earth. That is why He will place God given desires upon your heart! **(Psalm 37:4)**

I have an exercise for you. It's called the **(10,10) Full Convergence Exercise**. Get a piece of paper and make a list of all of the skills, talents, and God given gifts that you have (what is in your hand?).

On another piece of paper, make a list of your passions – things that flip your trigger, things that give you that ecstatic, warm fuzzy feeling! What are you passionate about? What do you like to do? These are your true passions! Write them down!

Got those 2 steps done? Good.

Now, make a list of EVERY job you have ever had on another piece of paper. Done? Now you are ready for the final step.

Using the **Full Convergence Map (Figure 1)**, plot each job, one by one on the map according to how your skills, talents, and gifts were used (scale of 1-10) and how passionate you were about that job (scale of 1-10).

For example, let's say you had a paper route as a young child. That job used few of your skills (maybe a 1 because you could ride a bike) and you weren't over the moon passionate about it (maybe a 2 because you had to get up early to do it). So you would plot that job (put an X) at the (1,2) location on the map as shown in **(Figure 1)**. Get it? Now you try. Take each job you listed previously and get them plotted on the map according to your skills, talents, gifts and passions. Make your own map if you need to; you get the idea!

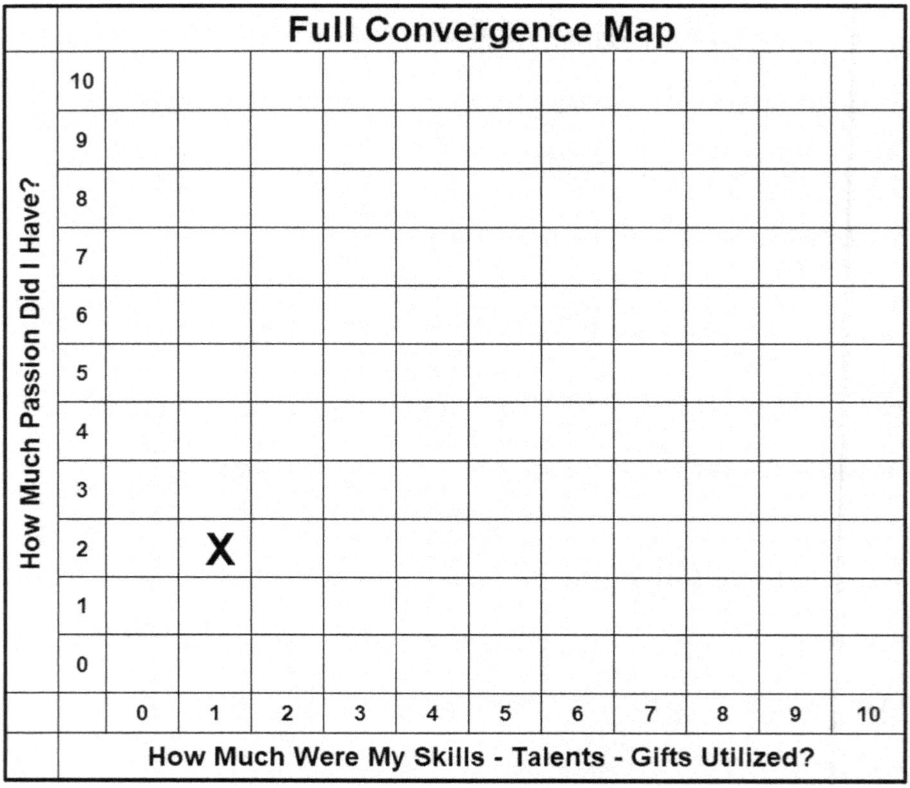

Full Convergence Map

How Much Passion Did I Have?		0	1	2	3	4	5	6	7	8	9	10
	10											
	9											
	8											
	7											
	6											
	5											
	4											
	3											
	2			X								
	1											
	0											

How Much Were My Skills - Talents - Gifts Utilized?

Figure 1 - Full Convergence Map

So, what is the point of this exercise? (drum roll please…..) To get to the (10,10) square on the map!!! (far upper right corner) – That is where you will be operating in FULL obedience and you will be operating out of the natural and in the supernatural! You see, when your passions are in FULL convergence with your skills, talents and gifts, you will be loving and experiencing life, you are in full obedience! You love getting up in the morning and moving your life forward! You love what you do and do what you love! You have found your "there"!

Therefore, everything you do from now on (education – jobs – where you live – etc) NEED to be in this (10,10) zone. FULL CONVERGENCE!!! That is where you will be most effective and that is where you will enjoy yourself the most, because you are operating in obedience and you are therefore operating in the supernatural! If you get this right, your life will never be the same! Find your (10,10) and live in obedience to what God wants for you! He put those desires on your heart and He gave you those skills. Now what do you plan to do with them?

Expect the supernatural in your life! God is the same today, yesterday and tomorrow. He never changes **(Malachi 3:6)**.

Surrender to obedience and live outside the natural!

Traveling Through The Gate

Quiet your heart and ask for a Word from God.

Ask Him what He wants you to do with your life! Receive, then practice obedience by giving it a try. God is patient, baby steps are OK!

Complete the Full Convergence Exercise!

Courageously Releasing Your Power

- Expecting Favor & Blessings -

I'm a child of the 70s, so I'm going to bring up Star Wars, the movie. May the force be with you! Remember that? Can you imagine if you had that kind of power? Like Obi-Wan Kenobi had with the Force? Well guess what... you do! In **(Eph 1:18-20)** it is written that you have the same power on the inside of you, that raised Christ from the dead! That is a LOT of power! Don't believe me? Look it up; that supernatural power is already on the inside of you, you just have to activate it and release it into your life.

I loved that scene in Star Wars where Obi Wan told those soldiers.... "these aren't the droids you are looking for". He was using the force, or the supernatural internal power of protection that we all have. Since I began to understand this power, I say the same thing when adversity comes against me, whether its sickness, negativity, the news media lies etc. I just say "I'm not the one you are looking for" and just like that, the problem disappears! It took a lot of work on my part and a lot of faith to really believe I had that kind of God given power on the inside of me. But now that I know the truth, that this supernatural power is real, I hang onto it likes it is gold.

Nothing can come against me now, and it is written that my enemies may come at me from one direction and flee from me in seven! **(Deut 28:7)** Embrace the knowledge of this power and use it wisely; it is a gift from God but it comes with a lot of responsibility. You now have the knowledge and the understanding about the power; it's up to you now to find the wisdom to use it. We will discuss knowledge, understanding and wisdom later in this book; but for now, let's continue to talk about releasing and activating this supernatural power.

You receive power once you receive the Holy Spirit into your life. The baptism of the Holy Spirit is a separate experience from salvation. It is a second encounter with God, when you receive power from on high. Even Jesus needed this power before he was able to start His ministry and He also told the disciples not to minister without this power from the Holy Spirit. If Jesus and the disciples needed this power, then how much more so do YOU need it? When I speak of your power, I am not talking about your "own" power in the flesh, but rather the power that you acquire when you receive the Holy Spirit into your life. This is a courageous step in your spiritual journey, but believe me, once you have the power of the Holy Spirit in your life, you will begin to wonder how you ever lived here on earth without it!

This power is one that is able to heal, to show you favor and abundance, and in the old testament, God described this power as the ability to get wealth **(Deut 8:18)** This wealth is not for yourself, as it is part of the abundance that I speak of. You can't give what you don't have and we are commanded to give. What you put out, you get back. So, learn to give so that you can receive. Courageously release your power to attract abundance and provision into your life! Learn to expect favor and blessings!

One of my favorite ways to introduce blessings to people is to tell the story called Mr. Jones Goes To Heaven. This story is told in *The Prayer of Jabez: Breaking Through to the Blessed Life* by Bruce

Wilkinson (you will find this title in the suggested reading section of this book) Here is the story:

There's a little fable about a Mr. Jones who dies and goes to heaven. Peter is waiting at the gates to give him a tour. Amid the splendor of golden streets, beautiful mansions, and choirs of angels that Peter shows him, Mr. Jones notices an odd-looking building. He thinks it looks like an enormous warehouse — it has no windows and only one door. But when he asks to see inside, Peter hesitates. "You really don't want to see what's in there," he tells the new arrival.

Why would there be any secrets in heaven? Jones wonders. What incredible surprise could be waiting for me in there? When the official tour is over he's still wondering, so he asks again to see inside the structure.

Finally Peter relents. When the apostle opens the door, Mr. Jones almost knocks him over in his haste to enter. It turns out that the enormous building is filled with row after row of shelves, floor to ceiling, each stacked neatly with white boxes tied in red ribbons.

"These boxes all have names on them," Mr. Jones muses. Turning to

Peter he asks, "Do I have one?"

"Yes, you do." Peter tries to guide Mr. Jones back outside. "Frankly," Peter says, "if I were you...." But Mr. Jones is already dashing toward the "J" aisle to find his box.

Peter follows, shaking his head. He catches up with Mr. Jones just as he is slipping the red ribbon off his box and popping the lid. Looking inside, Jones has a moment of instant recognition, and he lets out a deep sigh like the ones Peter has heard so many times before.

Because there, in Mr. Jones's white box, are all the blessings that God wanted to give to him while he was on earth...but Mr. Jones had never asked.

~

"Ask," promised Jesus, "and it will be given to you" **(Matthew 7:7)**. "You do not have because you do not ask" **(James 4:2)**. Even though there is no limit to God's goodness, if you didn't ask Him for a blessing yesterday, you didn't get all that you were supposed to have.

That's the catch — if you don't ask for His blessing, you forfeit those that don't come to you when you don't ask. Your heavenly Father is delighted to respond generously when His blessing is what you covet most!

Asking for blessings and expecting favor activates the release of supernatural power in your life. You must acknowledge favor and blessings out loud! There is empowerment in the tongue, so speak your blessings out loud! Proclaim and speak these blessings over your life. Claim them now!

Every morning when I get up, and my feet hit the ground, I stand facing east, taking in the morning sun, and I say "Thank you God for all of my blessings! If there is anyone out there who doesn't want theirs, send them to me! I'll take 'em!" You can borrow that 'ritual' if you would like, give it a try tomorrow morning when you wake up! Get ready to receive, because blessings will be headed your way! Take the ribbon off of your box in heaven! Those blessings are meant to be yours NOW, not something to find later after you return home.

Live in the supernatural, where favor and blessings begin to flow. Don't beg God to move, YOU move! He has given you the supernatural power to excel in all things; it's up to you whether you release that power into your life or not.

You say you will believe it when you see it? NO! You will only see it when you BELIEVE it. You have it backwards (most people do). Start believing that you already have it, nurture that belief with faith. Believe in the unseen. Expect victory and freedom. Remember the story of Moses (what do you have in your hand?) Courageously release your supernatural power and you will begin to see favor and blessings! This is the basis for manifestation and the Law of Attraction. You will be surprised how your life changes when you focus on releasing your God given power. Life becomes immensely more enjoyable when you release favor and blessings into your life!

While I'm on the subject of blessings, let's take a look at **(Deuteronomy 28)**. Did you know that there are 14 verses in the bible that are solely dedicated to your blessings? Let's travel back to the Old Testament and have a look!

Blessings for Obedience (Deuteronomy 28:1-14)

If you fully obey the Lord your God and carefully follow all his commands I give you today, the Lord your God will set you high above all the nations on earth. All these blessings will come on you and accompany you if you obey the Lord your God:

You will be blessed in the city and blessed in the country. The fruit of your womb will be blessed, and the crops of your land and the young of your livestock — the calves of your herds and the lambs of your flocks. Your basket and your kneading trough will be blessed. You will be blessed when you come in and blessed when you go out. The Lord will grant that the enemies who rise up against you will be defeated before you. They will come at you from one direction but flee from you in seven. The Lord will send a blessing on your barns and on everything you put your hand to. The Lord your God will bless you in the land he is giving you.

The Lord will establish you as his holy people, as he promised you on oath, if you keep the commands of the Lord your God and walk in obedience to him. Then all the peoples on earth will see that you are called by the name of the Lord, and they will fear you. The Lord will grant you abundant prosperity — in the fruit of your womb, the young of your livestock and the crops of your ground — in the land he swore to your ancestors to give you.

The Lord will open the heavens, the storehouse of his bounty, to send rain on your land in season and to bless all the work of your hands. You will lend to many nations but will borrow from none. The Lord will make you the head, not the tail. If you pay attention to the commands of the Lord your God that I give you this day and carefully follow them, you will always be at the top, never at the bottom. Do not turn aside from any of the commands I give you today, to the right or to the left, following other gods and serving them.

~

Ask God for a Word and believe that you receive it!

Courageously release your God given power and start expecting favor and blessings!

Traveling Through The Gate

Face east every morning, and face the sun. Give thanks to God for all of your blessings! Claim favor and protection over your life!

Speak out loud and release the supernatural power from the inside of you, commanding it to heal your soul and body!

Awakening to Spirit

- Reclaiming the Knowledge of Who You Are -

When you came to earth, you forgot who you were. That was by design; if you knew who you were and you knew your purpose when you got here, then where would the learning be? Where would the journey be? We have to seek, so we can find. We have to participate in life, not just have it handed to us. When we eventually figure how WHO we are and WHY we are here, we awaken to spirit and our life takes on a whole new meaning and direction!

God is Spirit and those who worship Him must worship Him in Spirit **(John 4:24)**. Worship means to "pay homage to", "to adore", "to revere", and the Greek word for Spirit is Pneuma, which means your "rational immortal soul". So, in order to fully worship our Creator, we must operate from our spirit and from our heart, not from our earth bound ego and our flesh.

You need to fully understand Spirit, Soul and Body. You need to get out of the flesh, because the Spirit gives life, the flesh counts for nothing **(John 6:63)**.

In **(Figure 2)**, you will see circles depicting the relationship between your Spirit, your Soul, and your Body. Your Spirit, the part of you that has a relationship with your Creator and operates in the supernatural, is depicted by the circle on the right (East). Your Soul, which is basically your personality governed by your mental state and emotions, is depicted as the 2 center circles (North & South). Your physical Body, which you can touch and see in a mirror, is depicted by the circle on the left (West).

Notice how these circles interact with each other. When your Spirit interacts (overlaps) with either your Mind or your Emotions, then you are operating from your HEART, which is a place of very HIGH vibration, where you can operate within the supernatural. When your Body interacts (overlaps) with either your Mind or your Emotions, then you are operating from your FLESH, which is a place of very LOW vibration, where you can only operate in the natural. (we will discuss energy and vibrations in another chapter)

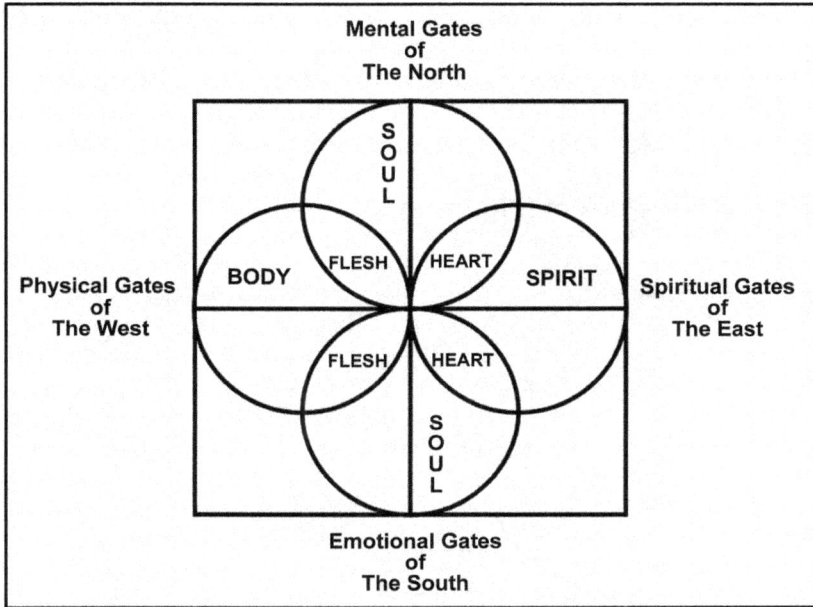

Figure 2 - Interactions of the Spirit, Soul & Body

Notice that your Spirit never interacts (overlaps) directly with your Body. This is because the natural and the supernatural are opposites and do not interact with one another. You can't be a blend of Heart and Flesh; you can't operate in the natural and at the same time operate in the supernatural. If you truly want to awaken to spirit, you must first come to the realization of who you truly are IN the spirit!

Furthermore, your thoughts and emotions must become one single force, for that is when you get the power to speak to the world, and

FAITH is produced. In other words, you have to feel (emotions) AND believe (thoughts) that what you are asking for, or manifesting has ALREADY happened! Your thoughts and emotions must become ONE single force. Have a look at **(Figure 3)**.

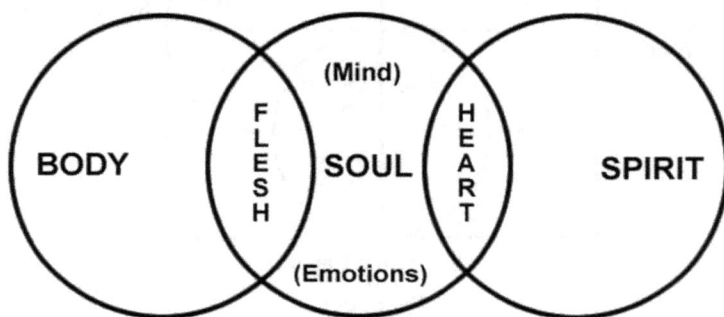

Figure 3 – Thoughts and Emotions of the Soul

It is FAITH that allows the release of your supernatural power which we have discussed previously, and this faith thereby allows you to command your Body to receive from the supernatural and to come into obedience with your Spirit. Faith then, is the BRIDGE between the Spirit and the Body **(Figure 4)**, and without this bridge (faith), you will not be able to operate fully in the supernatural or be awakened to spirit.

This process takes time, its not some overnight aha moment that you

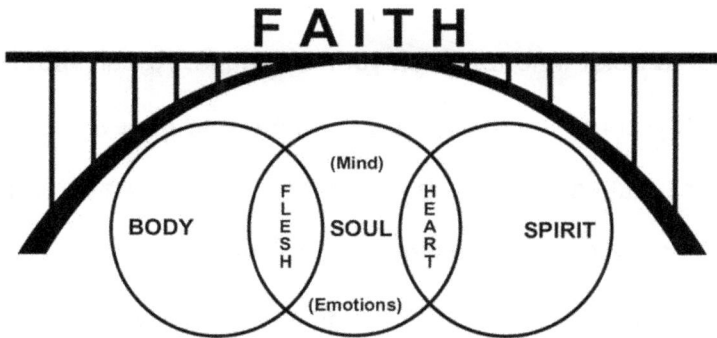

Figure 4 - The Bridge of Faith

"get", and you don't become instantly changed. A relationship with your Creator is the first step, learning and knowing who you are is the second step, and realizing you are a spiritual being having a human experience is the third step. This is a process, and it takes time.

God will never remove his anointing from you no matter how bad you screw up in the flesh. If you want proof of that, just study David, Elijah, Joseph and others in the bible who operated in their own strength time after time. Further realize that God has never had anyone qualified to work for Him yet, and YOU aren't going to be the first! Learn to live from your heart. God sees you in the spirit and wants you to connect with Him spirit to spirit! There is a good chance that He has been "knocking on your door" for some time, and you just need to open the door to receive! To prove this point, I challenge you to find some quiet time to revisit your entire life. Recall situations and challenges you have faced in your lifetime, and review the outcomes of these situations. Were you operating in your own strength when this happened? Or, do you now realize that you might have had a little help, from your Creator, your guides and your angels because the outcome was a miracle or a true blessing? Which was it? What life lessons where handed to you during these situations? Give this exercise some deep thought. If you need to quit reading for a moment, and work on this exercise, that is fine with me. Go ahead; I'll wait for you because this exercise will truly help you to awaken to spirit!

~

Once you realize that you are a spiritual being have a human experience, your thoughts begin to create your own reality because you begin to operate from the heart. Where your thoughts go, energy flows! So when your thoughts are originating from the heart space, then so does your energy! Is this making sense to you?

When you awaken to spirit, you begin to live in love and expansion. You are no longer constrained and held in the ego prison of the flesh.

You can no longer be confined. You can now begin to think for yourself and no longer act like a puppet or slave to your earthly environment. When you act as a puppet or slave to your environment, you are acting in the flesh and you have no spiritual identity. When you operate from the flesh, you easily become like everyone else – monkey see monkey do – you go along with the other sheep heading to slaughter. When you operate in the flesh, the World gives you your new normal and most people simply comply with this new normal because they are incapable of thinking for themselves! This choice of behavior is revolting! Who wants to be "normal" or worse yet "mediocre"? You came to this earth to SHINE, not get lost while operating in the flesh with a sea of puppets!

When you awaken to spirit, you become pure energy and love. The flesh operates out of self, ego, individuality and it's a very heavy existence that will weigh you down. The spirit operates as "One" with the Universe and operates as "One" with the collective. When you awaken to spirit, you live from your heart and you operate as light, high energy, your life becomes effortless, and your life is not held down by heavy rules and earthly constraints.

When you awaken to spirit and operate from the heart, you let go of earthly rules and authority. You become free, you do not stay trapped. You change the way you learn; you are no longer controlled by religion, institutions and man made concepts. When you awaken, you separate yourself from anything that is controlling you and keeping you bound in the flesh. When you awaken to spirit, you are able to unplug from the matrix and the role you have been playing, with your fellow actors in this fictitious movie on earth. Instead, you begin to enjoy "me" time – and not in a selfish way, but in a way that teaches you to "know thyself". You learn about who you really are, not who "they" told you that you were. (don't get me started on "they")

When you awaken to spirit, you learn to meditate from your heart, you learn to astral travel and you learn how to "get away" from the bondage you have been experiencing on earth. When you awaken to spirit, anything is possible – and I mean ANYTHING! You can dream without constraints. You begin to speak things into existence! People don't realize that when you say you "can" or you "can't" you are absolutely correct! You ARE what you speak and you must CHOOSE your words carefully!

When you awaken to spirit and you awaken to being "One" with nature and everything around you, you begin to realize that you ARE what you have been searching for all along! You realize that you and others who choose to operate from the heart are equal, you are all the same. You break away from the herd, so to speak, and you begin to honor your "downloads" and your new way of thinking. You plug in more deeply to your intuition, you begin to hear God speak to you in an audible voice and you begin to pay attention when your own inner voice (your God given power) speaks to you.

When you awaken to spirit, you begin to embrace the supernatural power inside of you. You begin to create your own reality and you begin to control your own destiny instead of it being controlled for you. Once you claim your supernatural power, and begin operating from the heart, your vision and imagination will begin to work full time for you!

Begin to embrace nature and begin to respect the natural medicine that is found in nature! Get outside more! Take in the sun, fresh air, drink from natural and fresh mountain springs and enjoy eating the food and fruits that nature naturally provides for you.

When you become awakened to spirit, you will begin to move beyond time. Do you ever notice people around you who never wear a watch, yet they somehow seem to be early or on time for all meetings or events with you? These people are living beyond the constraints of time. On the other hand, do you also notice the people who are arrogant enough to be constantly late to everything? Yes, I know some of those people too. Unfortunately, they are living in the flesh, constrained by this world and by time. They are so stuck in their flesh and ego that they think it is ok to make you wait for them while they choose to show up late. That is self centeredness and arrogance; that is where the ego and flesh will take you!

There is a much better way for you to operate! When you awaken to spirit, you realize that there is only now; you need to be present! Live in the eternal now! Forget about the past and the future, because neither of those will serve you for your higher good! When you are awakened to spirit, time no longer has a hold on you!

You want to operate in God's best. When you awaken to spirit and realize that we are all connected, you choose to operate from the heart, you begin to see the benefit of helping others and you begin to treat others as you want to be treated (not with arrogance and ego)! You begin to operate with unification not separation! You begin to operate without boundaries, and without walls. Remember what Jesus said in **(Matt 25:40)**? "Truly I say to you. In as much as you did it to one of these, the least of my brothers, you did it to Me". Then again in **(Matt 25:45)** "Truly I say to you. In as much as you did NOT do it to one of these, the least, nether did you do it to Me". Jesus is reminding us that we have a choice; a choice to operate in love from the heart, or to operate in ego from the flesh.

When you awaken to spirit, you become open to new things, new experiences, new people, new territories, new environments, new expansion, new opportunities, and new information. You choose to stay in harmony with nature because you begin to realize that Mother Earth is alive just as you are. And most importantly, you choose to seek and find fellow awakened souls and spirits while you remain here on earth. You become interested in learning, evolving and reaching for higher destinations. You become aware of abundance and realize that the Universe has plenty for everyone, and you realize that you should not live according to lack. When you awaken to spirit, you begin to realize your own heart truth through your own research;

you no longer receive or believe everything that people simply "tell you". You begin to think for yourself!

Awakening to spirit is a fun and healthy place to be. Live life like it's meant to be lived! Move out of the ego driven flesh and into the heart driven spirit!

Awaken to spirit and reclaim the knowledge of who you really are!

Traveling Through The Gate

Before you fall asleep at night, ask to be taken on a journey! Your body needs rest, but your spirit never sleeps. Travel back to spirit school at night, and ask to receive knowledge about who you really are! Ask to remember your dreams, and try to interpret them when you wake up in the morning!

The Emotional Gates of the South

Gate #4 - Love, Faith, Joy & Peace

- Forgive As You Have Been Forgiven -

Gate #5 - Goodness, Kindness & Gentleness

- How We Relate to Others -

Gate #6 - Absolve Yourself From Fear

- How to Stop Conforming to the World -

Love, Faith, Joy & Peace

- Forgive As You Have Been Forgiven –

Works of the flesh, or works of the spirit? Where are you headed? Our emotions can lead us to either operational standard, less we take heed in the Word from **(Gal 5:16-17)** Lets have a look at that scripture: "But I say, walk by the Spirit, and you will not carry out the desire of the flesh. For the flesh sets its desire against the Spirit, and the Spirit against the flesh; for these are in opposition to one another." Time for your free will exercise! Are you going to choose to walk in the spirit or walk in the flesh? Are you going to choose to live emotionally from the spirit or choose to live emotionally from the flesh? Lets read further on in the Word **(Gal 5:22-24)** " But the fruit of the Spirit is love, joy, peace, patience, kindness, goodness, faithfulness, gentleness, self-control; against such things there is no law. Now those who belong to Christ Jesus have crucified the flesh with its passions and desires."

As a favored and blessed child of God, you have received the fruits of the spirit and we are to walk in the spirit. Lets discuss a few of these "fruits" and see how this scripture is put together.

The Greek word for love is agape which means affection and benevolence which is further defined as an act of kindness and a willingness to do good. Therefore, we are to operate in the spirit in love. People in your environment should see this love IN you and feel this love IN you. We love, because He first loved us. **(1 John 4:19)** What ever you claim to believe should be seen in your life. You should wear this love on your sleeve!

The Greek word for faith is pistis which means moral conviction, truth itself, assurance and belief. Faith is spiritual and supernatural; it is a gift from God and as we have seen, serves as a bridge between Spirit and Body. Faith is believing without seeing and faith comes through hearing the Word of God. James said that faith without works is dead; this means that we have to take action in order for our faith to come to pass! Take a rudder on a boat for example. A boat HAS a rudder mounted to it, but as long as the boat sits at the dock, the boat cannot travel left, right or make any turns. It is only when the boat is moving, that the rudder makes any difference at all; same with an airplane. An airplane has a rudder, but as the airplane sits in the hanger, the rudder plays no role at all. Yet, when the airplane is in motion, and flying, the rudder acts to steer the airplane. Faith is YOUR rudder! Faith is what causes the spiritual to flow into the body. Faith is the bridge from spirit to body, but just like the boat and the airplane, you must take action and you must be in motion for the rudder (your faith) to have an effect on your direction! So James was right! Faith, without works (action) is dead. Everyone has a rudder, because everyone has faith, but to what measure are you using yours? Do you have some work to do here?

The Greek word for joy is chara which means cheerfulness, calm delight and gladness. If we choose to walk in the spirit, then we choose to walk in joy! People should be able to see the joy in our lives. In fact, I think if you are honest with yourself, you will admit that you actually gravitate towards joyful people. Am I right? I know I do. Joy attracts joy and good energy attracts other good energy. Spirit gravitates towards spirit. Live in the spirit and live in joy! You will then find people beginning to gravitate towards YOU! You should take that as a compliment. Its not that they want to suck the energy out of you like an energy vampire, they just want what you have and the smart ones know that if they hang out with you and your joy, that some of it will rub off on them! After all, the world is full of abundance and there is plenty of joy to go around for everyone. If you don't want yours, I'll take it! I LOVE living my life with the high vibration of joy!

The Greek word for peace is eirene which means quietness, rest, to join or bind together as one, especially that which has been broken, divided or separated. I think you will agree that we all could use some peace in the world right now. I think broken, divided and separated are the tips of the iceberg when describing the world we live in right now; won't you agree? There is a lot of underlying destruction and actions of others that will try to disrupt your peace, but only YOU are in charge of your peace. It too, is a gift of God, and we all need peace. But just as with joy, peace is abundant, you just have to receive it! And before you can receive it, you must ask for it, believe you have it, and start living it!

These fruits of the spirit are a great reminder of how God wants us to live and where he wants us to come from with regards to our emotions. I challenge you with an exercise to think of times when you needed love, faith, joy and peace in your life. What was going on that you were not able to receive these truths? What had you avoided so that love, faith, joy and peace could not fall into place naturally into your life? Your life might have hit a speed bump or taken a detour, but the fruits of the spirit are a road map for you to follow. It's never too late to pick up the pieces and start receiving these "fruits" into your emotional life. Take some time to give this exercise some thought. God is patient and he and your angels are standing by to help you. But, remember the rudder? Faith? You must take action before you will receive the help. You can't beg God to "fix it", you have to start the change and transformation yourself; and then, all the help you could ever imagine will jump on board with you. Enjoy the ride! You are protected!

Now, lets talk about a subject that no one wants to talk about.... forgiveness. I used to not like to talk about this subject too, until I studied **(Eph 4:32)** "Be kind to one another, tender-hearted, forgiving each other, just as God in Christ also has forgiven you." The Greek word for forgive is charizomal which means to grant as a favor, to pardon or to rescue. When Jesus died for you, He forgave you (before you were born), for everything that you were ever going to do, have done, or are going to do next week as well! Everything! Through this blatant and thorough act of forgiveness, He pardoned you and rescued you; He FORGAVE you! Now, if you were forgiven THIS much, for things you haven't even done yet, how much more do you think that YOU can forgive someone else? From my perspective, there is nothing you could say that would even make a good argument here. Read **(Eph 4:32)** again and if you still can't forgive someone who has wronged you, read it again.... and again.... and again.... until your spirit gets it! This is very important and it's a life changer for someone who is serious about "doing the work". There is no greater love than this forgiveness, when Jesus laid down His life for YOU. You need to forgive others, just as you have been forgiven! You are going to say, "but what about so and so who I did harm to and who I wronged?" Well, you can only ask for forgiveness, you can't make them give it to you. But, just as we have discussed here before, energies attract like energies. And, if you give it time, you will come to see that people will begin to forgive YOU as well, when they see you forgiving others. This isn't about keeping a score sheet, its about you taking responsibility for living in forgiveness, asking for forgiveness and giving forgiveness to others. You don't forgive because it's the right thing to do, you forgive because you were handed the ultimate in forgiveness by Jesus. THAT is why you forgive others!

Let me add one very important and final note on this topic of forgiveness. You MUST forgive YOURSELF also. If you are guilty of something and know that you made a bad decision or acted in an inappropriate way at some time, then you MUST forgive yourself! When you fail, and don't forgive yourself, your own self condemnation will hinder what God can do with your situation. Not forgiving yourself for your bad deeds or actions will lower your vibration and cause this gate to shut. Once the gate is shut, you are also shut out from love, faith, joy and peace. Think about that!

God forgave you long ago, you can't surprise Him with anything you have done or will do in the future. He just wants your heart and He wants you to live in abundance and fullness. He wants you to turn your heart towards Him. We all have love to give, but can you FORgive?

Live with love, faith, joy & peace! Forgive as you have been forgiven!

Traveling Through The Gate

Make a list of people you have wronged. Make a list of people that have wronged you! Release forgiveness and ask for forgiveness in return. Forgive yourself! Speak out loud that you are fogiving others, because God has forgiven you! Use the spiritual highway to send and receive messages! Keep your angels employed!

Goodness, Kindness & Gentleness

- How We Relate to Others -

Lets continue to study more fruits of the spirit, which is God's standard for life and how we can enter into God's best. As a reminder, here is **(Gal 5:22-23)** "But the fruit of the Spirit is love, joy, peace, patience, kindness, goodness, faithfulness, gentleness, self-control; against such things there is no law."

The Greek word for goodness is agathosune which means virtue or beneficence (high moral standards), a moral obligation to act for the benefit of others, and concerning the welfare of others. We need to have compassion for others as we operate in goodness. We do not know what others may be going through. We see people acting out all the time when situations or circumstances don't seem to be going "their way". Often in selfishness, self centeredness and feelings of entitlement, people will throw goodness out the window, as they act with only themselves in mind. This is a reminder that we always need to give thought as to what others may be going through at any given time. Many anger management classes, or other emotion based classes will teach "intellect over emotion". This is the very concept I am talking about. You never know what someone else may be going through, so when things don't go as you expect them to, try to not emotionally over react, and instead deal with the situation from the perspective of the moral obligation of goodness.

The Greek word for kindness is chrestotes which means moral behavior, excellence in character, or excellence in demeanor. When someone is operating in kindness, they may "pay it forward" for someone else, doing the very thing that someone else did for them. Kindness is repaid with kindness. An even better act of kindness is one that is done unconditionally, when you are not expecting anything in return. And still yet, an even better act of kindness is one which is performed anonymously, where the recipient doesn't even know that you were the one that did the kind deed for them! Think about that and give that a try! Be patient, the correct response to a situation is not always the easiest one. But once you decide to deliberately act with kindness, it will become a way of life for you, as you begin to put others first.

The Greek word for gentleness is praiotes which means meekness and humility. One of the best visualizations of gentleness is that of a mother dog handling her puppies after they are born. If you watch her, you will see how she works around them with gentleness even though she is much larger than they are and can crush several of them just by laying down. But, she is gentle. Also when she picks the puppies up in her mouth, have you ever observed how careful and gentle a mother dog is? Those jaws are strong enough to crush her puppy to pieces, but through gentleness, she handles them with love, goodness and kindness. Keep that in mind the next time you have a chance to be gentle with someone, be it physically or with words. Remember the actions of a mother dog with her puppies and see if you can change how you relate to others with gentleness.

While we are on the subject, lets talk about how we are to relate to others. In a nutshell, we are commanded to love our neighbor. We are commanded to carry ourselves with excellence and to offer God's best in all that we do. **(Col 3:23)** is one of my favorite scriptures and it says that "whatever you do, do your work heartily, as for the Lord rather than for men". We can easily get stuck in the flesh when we are surrounded by ungodly people or people who do not have our best interests in mind. We come across these circumstances all the time. But what helps me when I come up against these situations is to remember that I am to do my work and conduct my life with excellence because I'm serving God, not because I'm serving man. I therefore can let go of all expectations (which lead to disappointment by the way) and just live my life or do my job "heartily, as for the Lord". This means that you should not attack what you hate, because that will only attract more negativity, but rather you should promote what you love! When we promote what we love, we enter into the fruits of the spirit and we begin to operate in peace, prosperity, wonder and brilliance! I challenge you to think about this concept the next time you find yourself "stuck" in a situation that is... shall we say.... unpleasant! If you are the new person on the job and you are given the task to clean toilets, then instead of getting disgruntled and entering into a negative pattern of thinking, clean those toilets "heartily, as for the Lord"!! Are you laughing? Or at least smiling? I think you get my point!

We are to do everything in God's Best. **(Gal 5:25)** says that if we live by the Spirit, we should also walk by the Spirit. We are not to become boastful, challenging one another, or envying one another. Clean those toilets for the Lord and do it in God's best!

How else can we better relate to others? In keeping with goodness, kindness, and gentleness, we also need to understand the difference bet empathy and sympathy. It's easy to get the two confused.

Feeling sympathy for someone is a positive energy because it's a surface-level acknowledgment of someone's feelings or a situation that they're going through. Being sympathetic is about saying, "I hear you, and I value what you're feeling." We definitely need to demonstrate this more in society. With the concept of sympathy, it is about being "close to or with," and compassion with sympathy allows you to think about a situation but remain at a safe distance, so your emotional state of mind probably isn't profoundly compromised when acting out of sympathy.

Sympathy is primarily about observation and an acceptance that someone else is going through a challenging experience. It can amount to "feeling sorry" for someone, which is an acknowledgment of a situation. It's not a concept that requires someone to experience the emotion that another person is going through. Sympathy is "feeling WITH," instead of "feeling FOR" another person. Therefore, acting in sympathy provides a natural detachment from the situation.

Empathy, on the other hand, is a much broader, more intense emotional reaction to a situation that another person may be going through. Acting with empathy may bring up a range of emotions which you may find difficult to manage, because you are now taking on the actual feelings of the person.

This is the critical difference between empathy and sympathy – instead of feeling WITH someone, you are now feeling FOR them when you act with empathy. You are experiencing a fraction of their emotions and feelings because you see things from their perspective. You are putting yourself in their shoes, so to speak.

So, is it better to act with sympathy or empathy in a given situation? This all depends on what your comfort level is and who you are dealing with. If you have lived through or struggled with a similar situation, then you most likely will respond with empathy. This approach will help you better connect with an individual who is going through a situation that you have already experienced. The next time you have a chance to choose sympathy or empathy in a given situation, stop and give thought to which direction you are coming from. Ask yourself why you are choosing the response that you are, and later, given the result of the situation, further ask yourself if you made the best choice. This too, is a process and you need to be patient with yourself as you "do the work".

Another way that we relate to others is how we speak to them. We spiritually have to understand the nature of the tongue and the empowerment of words. Words can build up others, by encouraging, mentoring and teaching, but they can also tear down others when we choose to gossip or belittle. We should relate to others out of goodness, and we should look to the interests of others. **(Phil 2:4)**

Live with goodness, kindness, and gentleness in your heart! Be aware of how you relate to others!

Traveling Through The Gate

Pay it forward today. Do a kind gesture for someone. Start with a small deed and increase your participation as it becomes natural for you!

Get outside and look at all living things as something that you are able to nurture!

6

Absolve Yourself From Fear

- How to Stop Conforming To the World -

The acronym FEAR stands for False Evidence Appearing Real. That's right, false evidence. Doing what? Appearing real. Want me to say it again? Fear, is false evidence appearing real! If you can commit that statement to memory, you should be able to catch yourself the next time you are faced with a potentially fearful situation.

Where does fear come from? I believe that when people are out of balance emotionally, they are more susceptible to situations causing fear in their lives and they are more likely to follow a herd mentality, a monkey see – monkey do mentality, and drive themselves off into a ditch (figuratively) without even realizing how they got there. They are totally unable to think for themselves, so they are easily manipulated and their behaviors can become very transparent and predictable.

One way to cause fear in an individual is to "sound the alarm". To basically put someone in a state of uncertainty, causing them to worry that something unpleasant or dangerous might happen to them or someone they love. Another way to cause fear in an individual is to create a feeling of panic which is a state where most people cannot think clearly and cannot make a good decision as to how to act or react given a certain situation. A third way to cause fear in an individual is through intimidation; to deliberately make someone fearful, uncertain and submissive so that they will do what you want.

If you believe that your power is outside of you, then you will experience severe consequences in your lifetime. If you believe that this power belongs to something or someone else, then that "thing" will hold dominion over your life. However, once you come to the realization of who you truly are, and you realize that your power comes from your spirit within, you will then be able to live in an ascended and rich way. When you walk in the spirit and live supernaturally, you actually can manifest your outside circumstances from within. When you believe that outside events and people have control over your life, you are kept from living the richness that is rightfully yours. You are blessed to be able to live in the spirit, do not choose to live in fear!

One of the best biblical stories that demonstrates spirit over fear is the story of David and Goliath which you can read about in **(1 Samuel 17)**. In short, a great Philistine giant named Goliath, which stood at over nine feet tall, came to the front of the Philistine battle line each day for forty days and mocked the Israelites and their God. Goliath called to them to fight, but King Saul and the Israelites were scared and fearful and did nothing. (F.E.A.R. – False Evidence Appearing Real) You will read about how the people were terrified and how they actually retreated and fled in fear. Then David shows up! And, he agrees to take on this giant! His people try to dress him in bulky armor and dress him in warrior gear, but David remarks that he doesn't want that protection of clothing and armor because he is not used to it and isn't comfortable wearing it. What was he comfortable with then? His God, and his God alone. How is THAT for taking a stand? And just because I love this story so much, here is **(1 Samuel 17:45)** "Then David said to the Philistine, "You come to me with a sword, a spear, and a javelin, but I come to you in the name of the Lord of hosts, the God of the armies of Israel, whom you have taunted." And, if you know the rest of the story, you also know that David stood before this giant with his sling shot and a few rocks. (hold my beer!) Oh my! That just puts a smile on my face! I've included a picture of the story here for you just so you can get the visual. Would you have been among those that fled? Or, would you have had enough faith in your God and WHO you are, to be able to do what David did? I think you know the rest of the story; David smacked that giant between the eyes with a rock and the giant fell to the ground and died.

This story of David and Goliath is a lesson of courage, faith, and overcoming what seems impossible. Just know that any circumstance (giant) in front of you is never bigger than the God who lives inside of you! **(Psalm 91)** reminds you of the great spiritual protection that is placed over you at all times. Read it over and over, memorize it if you have to, and keep it near. No harm or plague shall come near your dwelling! Speak that out loud anytime you come up against a "giant". Your "dwelling" is your body which is protected by your faith and your walk in the spirit!

(1 John 4:18) says that there is no fear in love; but perfect love casts out fear, because fear involves punishment and the one who fears is not perfected in love. Who doesn't want to live in perfect love? Our God is perfect Divine Love - the purest of love! And, he invites us to receive and experience that love, therefore if God is for you, who can be against you? **(Romans 8:31)** And finally, in **(Phil 4:8)** we are told to keep our thoughts pure and without negativity: " Finally, brethren, whatever is true, whatever is honorable, whatever is right, whatever is pure, whatever is lovely, whatever is of good repute, if there is any excellence and if anything worthy of praise, dwell on these things.

Step out of fear, and step into divine love! Turn off worldly pleasures **(Prov 21:17)** and turn on spiritual pursuit **(Gal 5:16)**. In this way you will live a protected life and you will no longer conform to this world. You have to find YOUR normal, not live by what others tell you your normal should be. Be bold! Stand for the Truth that lives inside of you!

Dare to be different! Step out of the mold! God didn't create you to be timid, and you didn't courageously come to have a human experience on earth so that you could walk around with your tail between your legs, whimpering in fear!

Stop caring what others think. Agree to disagree if you have to, but STAND! Be ready to tell others why you believe what you do!

(1 Peter 3:15) Give others a reason for the hope that is IN you. Stand in your faith and stand in the knowledge of WHO you are! You are a blessed, favored and protected child of the most high! **(Col 3:2)** says we are to set our minds on the things above, not on the things that are on earth! God is your source! If you agree with that, and truly believe that, then NOTHING in this world can come against you! **(Rom 8:31)** There is absolutely NOTHING to fear!

Instead of conforming to the world and doing what others tell you to do all the time, try stepping out on new adventures each week! Go learn something new! Don't let people tell you that you can't do that, or that you are incapable, or that you aren't smart enough! Blow that off! YOU have the strength of God inside of you! **(Phil 4:13)** Don't be a robot, a conforming puppet or jump off a cliff just because others

are doing it! Stand for the Truth! You are NOT a sheep heading to

Stop Conforming To The World			
Put Off	Scripture	Put On	Scripture
Anger	Prov 29:22	Self-Control	Gal 5:22-23
Conceit	1 Corin 4:7	Others	Phil 2:3
Critical	Gal 5:15	Kindness	Col 3:12
Discontent	Heb 13:5	Contentment	1 Tim 6:8
Disobedience	1 Samuel 12:15	Obedience	Deut 11:27
Earthly Desires	1 Peter 2:11	Spiritual Desires	Titus 2:12
Evil Thoughts	Matt 15:19-20	Pure Thoughts	Phil 4:8
Flesh Motives	1 Samuel 16:7	Spirit Motives	1 Corin 10:31
Following Crowd	Prov 1:10	Trust In God	Prov 3:7
Gossip	1 Tim 5:13	Edifying Speech	Eph 4:29
Hatred	Matt 5:21-22	Love	1 Corin 13:3
Inhospitable	1 Peter 4:9	Hospitable	Romans 12:13
Jealousy	Gal 5:26	Trust	1 Corin 13:4
Lack of Love	1 John 4:7-8, 20	Love	John 15:12
Losing Temper	Prov 25:28	Self-Control	Prov 16:32
Not Doing Best	Prov 18:9	God's Best	Col 3:23
Pride	Prov 16:5	Humility	James 4:6
Self Entitlement	James 2:1-9	Loving Others	Luke 6:31
Selfishness	Phil 2:21	Self-Denial	John 12:24
Stinginess	1 John 3:17	Generosity	Prov 11:24-25
Strife	Prov 13:10	Peace	James 3:17
Temporal Values	Matt 6:19-21	Eternal Values	2 Corin 4:18
Unbelief	Heb 3:12	Faith	Heb 11: 1,6
Unfaithfulness	Prov 25:19	Faithfulness	Luke 16:10-12
Unforgiving	Mark 11:26	Forgiving	Col 3:13
Ungratefulness	Romans 1:21	Gratefulness	Eph 5:20
Worldly Pleasures	Prov 21:17	Spiritual Pursuits	Gal 5:16
Worry Fear	Matt 6:25-32	Trust	1 Peter 5:7
Your Way	Prov 27:1	God's Way	James 4:14-16

Table 1 - Put Off and Put On Scriptures

slaughter, you are a KILLER sheep! You have supernatural power!

I challenge you to study the scriptures in **(Table 1)**. Learn, according to scripture, the behaviors that you should "put off" and the behaviors that you should "put on". Stop conforming to the world!

Take the time to review these scriptures and understand the meaning behind them. Then, choose a few that you think pertain to you personally and try making those changes in your thinking and in your actions. Start living in the spirit and not in the flesh! This too, is a process, but once you understand what God wants for you, each day of change and transformation will become easier for you!

Absolve yourself from fear, and stop conforming to the world!

Traveling Through The Gate

Stop watching the news and turn off your TV, you don't deserve to be lied to. Find something positive to do with your time!

Go outside, explore nature. Quiet your mind and tune into the wind, the sounds, and your surroundings! Find the positive no matter where you are! Learn something new every day!

The Physical Gates of the West

Gate #7 - Servitude and Gratitude

- It's a Choice to Give and Receive -

Gate # 8 - Understanding Self-Control & Balance

- Actions and Consequences -

Gate # 9 - Expecting Miracles

- Sowing the Seed and Reaping the Harvest -

Servitude and Gratitude

- It's a Choice to Give and Receive -

We are to live a life of servitude and gratitude and we are to give thanks for everything, always. It is written that we are to "serve" with "thanksgiving". **(Phil 4:6-7)** We are to believe in the law of abundance and prosperity; you can't give what you don't have! Does that make sense to you? We are to serve others when we have the chance, and we are to be good receivers as well!

Some of you were taught by the world and by religion that it "is better to give than to receive", so I want to spend some time here to address that falsehood. This concept of "better to give" has come through false religious teaching and stems from **(Acts 20:35)** where Paul said, "remember the words of the Lord Jesus, that He Himself said, 'It is more blessed to give than to receive'."

First of all, there is no where in the bible where Jesus is recorded as saying this. Although, we must remain aware that Jesus said a LOT of things that were not recorded in the bible; there was simply too many of His works to capture. This truth is stated in **(John 21:25)** But on with my point…. The first thing you should notice is that the word "better" is not even used in this scripture. This too, became a translation that was used in some religious teachings. The actual word used in the original Greek manuscript is "blessed".

The Greek word for blessed is makarios which means happy, well and fortunate. This Greek word makarios is also the one used in The Beatitudes **(Matt 5)** where Jesus is recorded as saying "Blessed are they who….." over and over again. Never once, in The Beatitudes, does Jesus say blessed are those who give. Please make a mental note of that!

The Greek word for give is didomi which means to bring forth, commit, grant, offer, put, provide, and it also means smite with the hand or strike with the palm of the hand. Smite and strike? I did not know that! As an aside, I'm sure we can all think of someone that we would like to "give" something too! Ha ha ha! OK, sorry for the detour, on with my point.

The Greek word for receive is lambano which means to take, to get hold of, accept, attain (reach or achieve finality), catch, have, hold, and obtain (acquire, get possession of, established).

Do you see what I see here? It is more blessed to give than receive actually means that giving is a fortunate ability that we have that grants us the feeling of well being and happiness, and that this giving is what we should do RATHER than taking, attaining or holding on to something (hoarding)! The scripture is not teaching that receiving is bad, it's telling you not to hoard, keep, or hold on to what you receive. If you don't follow this, go back and re-read the Greek definitions of Blessed, Give and Receive.

Would you like a football analogy? The quarter back throws the ball (gives) to the receiver who catches it (receives). Does the receiver then throw the ball to someone else? No! Once he catches it, he has "received" it. He holds on to it. He hoards the ball! If its our team that is catching the ball, we hope he runs all the way to the end zone with it scoring a touchdown! Wait, so after catching, holding, hoarding and running – he is able to "give" points to the team? Hey! So you CAN give back after you receive! I think in the non football world, we call that "paying it forward".

It's also OK to receive a compliment without giving one back. This is very difficult, as we have been conditioned and taught in society that when someone says something nice to us, we are to say something similar back. I'm not sure how all of that started, but just know that it's ok to simply receive! If someone pays you a compliment, (nice shirt!) its fine to receive; just smile, and say "thank you". Practice receiving when the situation presents itself!

Learn to receive, and understand that this is a learned process, as we have been taught that receiving is not accepted as a "norm". So give it a try, and also learn to receive and pay it forward to someone else! Have you ever heard of give and take? What goes around, comes around? Yep, I think you've got it! Ask for help from your Creator and your angels while you are working on giving AND receiving. Your angels liked to be employed!

Once God gives you a gift, He does not take it away – But some people are unable to receive gifts from God because they have hardened hearts. Their heart is hardened because while they know their Creator, they refuse to participate in the life He has given them. Their heart could also be hardened because they cannot hear or see the call that God has placed on their life **(Mark 8:17-18)**

After I received the Word of Truth from God, I was excited to show others; so they could see what I could see! I used to ask God to "send me" and "use me". He later told me He would use me when I became usable. Well, all-righty then! Ouch! The good news is that I finally became usable and now I live a Godly life of servitude and gratitude; giving AND receiving! And now recently, when I was called to write this book, I was obedient and took on the task with joy!

Did you know that your job is actually a form of service? A way to give? GOD is your source **(Eph 6:5-8)** not your job, so you should serve and live your purpose through your job. I know you are thinking "no way, how am I supposed to do that?" Well, the answer can be found in **(Col 3:23)** where it is written that we should "Work as to the Lord, not for men". You can also give and receive through generosity! It is written in Proverbs that "the blessed soul will be made fat; he who waters will also drink fully". **(Prov 11:25)** So, you see that when you refresh others, you too will be refreshed! Learn to serve others!

Live from the heart, not the flesh. Give unconditionally and give anonymously; don't boast about your giving. Serve unconditionally, and don't ask for anything back after serving. It is written in **(Luke 6:38)** "Give, and it will be given to you: good measure, pressed down, shaken together, and running over will be put into your bosom. For with the same measure that you use, it will be measured back to you." Some call this the Law of Attraction! What you put out, you get back! Start giving and living from your heart and watch the abundance flow right back to you! And finally, remember what Jesus said about servitude? Whatever you did for one of the least of these brothers and sisters of mine, you did for me. **(Matt 25:40)** When you serve others, you are traveling through the MAIN gate!

Be grateful for the little things in life and never take anything for granted. Have you ever asked yourself why we "give thanks" ONCE a year during the Thanksgiving holiday? That always struck me as kind of strange, as I give thanks every minute of every day. I live in constant gratitude, I do not "give thanks" only once a year. I often tell people that I "do" Thanksgiving EVERY day! Living in gratitude will give you a LOT of joy and peace. Start paying attention to that today!

Give thanks for ALL of your blessings. If you don't know what those are, then you need to put yourself in "timeout" and give this some serious thought! Every morning when I get up, I stand facing east, looking into the sun, and I say "Thank you God, for all of my blessings, if someone out there doesn't want theirs, I'll take 'em!" I "give thanks" every day, the minute I get out of bed and my feet hit the ground! If you research the home architecture of the Native American Indians, you will find that they built their homes with the main door facing east! It was their morning ritual to stand in their doorway, facing the sun in the east, every day to give thanks to their Creator and to receive blessings. Check out **(Isaiah 60:1)** "Arise, shine; for your light has come! And the glory of the LORD is risen upon you." Oh, what a beautiful scripture!

You too, should continuously give thanks to the Lord for all of YOUR blessings and what He has done for you! God will still use you, in spite of your circumstances. Nothing is too big for your God! Receive from Him and Serve Him! **(Exodus 4:10-11)**

Live your life with servitude and gratitude! Choose to give AND receive!

Traveling Through The Gate

Practice the unconditional giving of your time, efforts or any physical items!

Practice listening and receiving! If someone pays you a compliment, receive it and say thank you!

Practice being of service to others today!

8

Understanding Self-Control & Balance

- Actions and Consequences -

Learn from your mistakes. Remember when you were a young child and your parents warned you about putting your hand on the hot stove? Some of you didn't listen and got burned! I was one of the ones that didn't listen. But you can rest assured that I didn't later choose to put my OTHER hand on the stove! You learn early on, that your actions have consequences!

You will notice fake people around you who choose to speak one way, but act another. Actions and words reflect what is in your heart, so live from your heart (not your flesh) and let people see the REAL you! God sees you in the spirit! How do the people in your environment see you?

If you have ever seen Dr. Phil, you will know that he often teaches "you choose the behavior, you choose the consequence". How true is that? We all have chosen behaviors (good and bad) and we all have had to live with the consequences of our actions! But, when you understand the life lessons that we learn along our journey, you will understand that none of these lessons have ever happened to you in vain.

When facing a situation and "free will" comes knocking at your door, you must practice self- control. "Whoever has no rule over his own spirit [no self-control] is like a city broken down, without walls." (**Prov 25:28)** The Greek word for self-control is egkrateia which means restraint and temperance. If you don't act with self-control, you will be out of balance!

Seek and you will find. Some times when we seek, we will find and experience the opposite of what we thought we were looking for! Our path will often take us in the opposite direction so that we will seek, find, and enhance the "desire" which God has placed upon our heart. Once we have that God given desire planted firmly in our heart, then we can take action towards our goal, and begin to seek, then follow our life purpose! Remember the discussion of the boat rudder and airplane rudder in an earlier chapter of this book? When we seek, we are taking action, we are moving, and that is when our rudder (faith) can direct our path!

Sometimes when we are tempted **(1 Corin 10:13)**, we find ourselves heading off in the wrong direction. But, c'mon! You were born with the innate knowledge of right v. wrong. You were also born with free will which gives you the option to "choose" your action. Choose right! Choose life! Choose obedience through the reading, studying and doing of the Word! Temptations are from the flesh and will destroy you; tests are from God and will cause you to grow! Read that again!

Sometimes we have to be pushed out of balance (off center) in order to get back into balance. When I speak of balance I am referring to your state of being – you are either living with the world (through the flesh) or living with the spirit (through the heart). You are out of balance when you are acting with self centeredness, arrogance, low self esteem, self focus, interrupting and talking over people, insinuating that what they have to say is not important to you. You are out of balance when you begin looking to your own interests instead of to the interests of others. Have you ever seen a hamster get stuck on the edge of his wheel after running on it? He spins round and round until he is finally flung off into the shavings! This can also happen to us if we choose to live out of balance in the world. You will find better love, joy and peace if you stay in the center of your wheel, where you can watch things go on around you while you remain centered, balanced and unaffected!

Remember the Medicine Wheel that we spoke of at the beginning of the book? The Medicine Wheel is sometimes depicted with a pearl at the center which represents centering and balance; the pearl represents the purity of the Creator within each of us. God is your strength and God is your source **(Eph 6:5-8)** Choose to stay centered and balanced! Once you are aligned and centered, God can use you, not when you are lopsided and out of balance!

Live your life with self-control and balance! Understand that your actions have consequences!

Traveling Through The Gate

Make a list of (5) situations where your (good or bad) actions had measurable consequences! Describe how you were in balance or out of balance for each of them!

For each situation, list some actions or behaviors that would have demonstrated a more balanced approach!

Expecting Miracles

- Sowing the Seed and Reaping the Harvest -

Miracles! One of my favorite topics! First of all, YOU are a miracle! Have you ever given thought to that? Have you ever thought about how or why you came into existence? Who brought you here and why? To answer that, you came from seed, just like every other living thing out there in the Universe. Your body came from the seed of your parents and your spirit came from God **(Ecle 12:7)** I won't get into depth, because THAT is another book, but stop if you need to and reflect on the miracle that is YOU. You are here for a reason, you chose to come here as spirit to have a human experience, and hopefully by now, you have started to see a glimpse of your purpose in life.

You must understand the concept of sowing and reaping. Planting and harvesting. Farmers plant seed (sow) and then later harvest their crop (reap). In the same way, God sows seed into your heart and the harvest is fruit; especially the fruits of the spirit which we have discussed in an earlier chapter of this book.

To further explain, let me share with you one of Jesus' famous stories – The Parable Of the Sower **(Matt 13:3-8)**:

"Behold, a sower went out to sow. And as he sowed, some [seed] fell by the wayside; and the birds came and devoured them. Some fell on stony places, where they did not have much earth; and they immediately sprang up because they had no depth of earth [no roots]. But when the sun was up they were scorched, and because they had no root they withered away. And some fell among thorns, and the thorns sprang up and choked them. But others fell on good ground and yielded fruit: some a hundredfold, some sixty, some thirty.

Because Jesus often spoke the mysteries of the Kingdom and miracles in parables, He had to further explain this one because the disciples were still not "getting it". I missed it the first time I read it too, so here is the explanation of The Parable Of the Sower - Everyone who hears the Word and does not understand it is like the seed that fell by the wayside. The Word landed in their hearts, but was quickly removed by the enemy. The one hearing the Word and immediately receiving it with joy, is like the seed landing on stony places. But the belief does not have good roots, so it lasts for a short time only, then disappears. The one who hears the Word, but then remains in the world, conforming to what others are anxiously doing, is like the seed that fell among the thorns. The thorns, like weeds, sprang up and choked out the Word, making it of no affect to the believer. Lastly, the one hearing the Word, while understanding it, while beginning to produce fruit, is like the seed that fell on good ground [fertile soil].

So, God sows the seed and YOU reap the harvest. But, the harvest that you reap fully depends on the "type of soil" in your heart. Did you notice that only 1 in 4 scenarios had a favorable outcome? Where seed is sown (planted) into good soil (your heart)? That is a true miracle!

The Greek word for miracle is semeion which means an indication, a supernatural sign, token or wonder. So, when you ever ask God to show you a "sign", you are actually asking Him to show you a miracle! Did you know that? Is your heart open enough to notice such a "sign" or to even receive a miracle if He sent you one? Get ready!

One of the biggest miracles I ever experienced was getting to meet one of my guardian angels Lehahiah, the 34th name of God. He came to me in a dream about two years ago. Once we met, my belief and faith soared and soon after, my world became full of "signs". My awareness of synchronicities in my life amplified one hundred fold. I began to receive signs through numbers, coins, and feathers just landing at my feet or in my path. My dreams and visions became more vivid, and every time I questioned ANYTHING, I got one of those signs again. The angel(s) and my Creator were constantly telling me that they were near and right beside me through these synchronicities. I became much bolder and I had more courage than I ever had, to move forward, working for the Lord not for men, and to reach out with more love for others! About 8 months after meeting Lehahiah, he told me to start the Prison Outreach. So I did! If you recall, I dedicated this book to him because he was the one who came to me 1 month ago and told me to write it! I now operate in full obedience (ironically Lehahiah is the "Angel of Obedience" – imagine THAT) and I do what I'm told in the spirit without questioning it. I do that because I now know that I am driven by Divine Power. I now EXPECT miracles, and I live my life with tremendous blessings, favor and love. I want this for YOU too, so open your eyes, and do the work! I mean it when I tell you that you won't be disappointed!

I've been open to receiving messages through the miracle of dreams for most of my life. It's always been the best way for God and his angels to speak to me. It can happen to you too! Remember Jacob's dream when he saw the ascending and descending angels? It is written that God will speak to you in dreams. Check out **(Job 33:14-15)**. "For God may speak in one way, or in another, yet one does not perceive it. In a dream, in a vision of the night, when deep sleep falls upon men, while slumbering on their beds, then He opens the ears of men, and seals their instruction." Before you go to sleep each night, ask God and your angels for help remembering your dreams. Ask for help receiving, remembering and discerning the spiritual messages that are given to you. Soon, you will be experiencing this miracle for yourself!

You won't find your life purpose and you won't be able to be on the spiritual highway with angels ascending and descending until you have God's seed planted firmly on good soil in your heart and you begin to expect miracles! Once you start the journey of doing the work, keep it all in motion! Keep giving and receiving! Keep living in servitude and gratitude! Open your eyes and keep living with and noticing signs, wonders and miracles all around you!

If you want to own your own business, sow into the businesses, community and situations that present themselves to you. Sow into the lives of OTHER people! Learn, apply the knowledge, then reap the harvest! Remember, if you refresh others, you TOO will be refreshed. What ever it is that you want to do in life, do it for others first and then reap the harvest for yourself! This is supernatural and the ultimate in sowing and reaping! Do nothing in your own power (flesh), but utilize the power of your spirit so that all be the Glory to God. **(John 5:30)**

Referring to Jesus, "as He is so are WE in this world" **(John 4:17)**. We are to sow and reap the harvest just as He taught us to. In **(John 14:12)**, Jesus told his disciples to do greater works than He did. You are His disciple TOO! So YOU are to do greater works than He did! You are to sow, reap the harvest and expect miracles to happen in your life!

Remember when God asked Moses what was in his hand? **(Exodus 4:2)** And Moses answered "a shepard's staff"? God corrected him and said, "NO! That is the Staff of God"!! So, I have to ask you, what Divine Tools are YOU blessed with? What is in YOUR hand?

Expect miracles in your life! Sow seed on good soil and reap a bountiful harvest!

Traveling Through The Gate

Try sending something out (sow) into the Universe! Expect miracles in return!

Positive thoughts, prayers, and gratitude are a good start. See what you get back. Give it time! Remember, you have help. Keep your angels employed!

Are you sowing on fertile soil? Describe.

The Mental Gates of the North

Gate # 10 - Knowledge, Understanding, and Wisdom

- The Keys to Life -

Gate # 11 - Victory in Healing

- Illness, Despair, and Poverty Mindsets -

Gate #12 - Raising Your Vibration

- Renewing Your Mind -

Knowledge, Understanding, & Wisdom

- The Keys to Life -

When you operate from the flesh and the ego, your thoughts become, "what I need to do", "what I have to do" and "what I should do". When you are operating from knowledge, understanding and wisdom, in the spirit, your thoughts are filled instead with aspirations and inspirations from God!

Knowledge can be defined as facts, information, things recovered from memory. As a disciple and child of God, you are instructed to gain knowledge through the Word and through careful study of the bible **(John 8:31-32)**. Your faith is based on knowledge and it is through this knowledge of God that Truth is revealed to you; this scripture says that it is the Truth that will set you free. I have JN832 on my license plate. It is one of my favorite scriptures! The knowledge of God is also mentioned in **(Prov 9:10)** which says "The fear of the Lord is the beginning of wisdom, and the knowledge of the Holy One is understanding."

So what exactly is understanding? Understanding is the lens through which we see the dynamics that exist around us. Understanding is the what, why, and how that produces principles of meaning and reason. Understanding is that which sheds light on a situation. **(Ps 119:130)**

"Trust in the Lord with all your heart, And lean not on your own understanding; In all your ways acknowledge Him, and He shall direct your paths. Do not be wise in your own eyes; Fear the Lord and depart from evil." **(Prov 3:5-7)** "The fear of the LORD is the beginning of wisdom; all those who [have the knowledge of God] and practice His commandments have a good understanding." **(Ps 111:10)** This concept is repeated again in **(Eph 1:17)**: "May [God], the Father of glory, give to you the spirit of wisdom and revelation in the knowledge of Him."

So lets be clear about what it means to "Fear the Lord", because many people are confused by what this means. To "fear" the Lord means to respect, to love, to honor, to revere, to worship, to adore, to approach Him with boldness, confidence and thankfulness. There is nothing scary about "fearing" the Lord. This is a positive term and should always be used in a positive light.

Wisdom is defined as the principle which is applied to a situation; an action, explanation or interpretation. "But the wisdom that is from above is first pure, then peaceable, gentle, willing to yield, full of mercy and good fruits, without partiality and without hypocrisy." **(James 3:17)**

Charles Spurgen, a well known and influential preacher from the 1800's once said, "Wisdom is the right use of knowledge. To know is not to be wise. Many men know a great deal, and are all the greater fools for it. There is no fool so great a fool as a knowing fool. But to know how to use knowledge is to have wisdom." I'll repeat that, you are said to have wisdom, when you demonstrate that you know how to use knowledge! If you want to spend time learning more about wisdom, spend time studying the entire book of Proverbs, and see how you can apply those truths to your life today!

Let me try to put knowledge, understanding, and wisdom into a practical application for you… Lets talk about gravity. You probably have knowledge about gravity and know it to be a force that attracts two bodies toward each other, and a force that causes things to fall toward the ground. If I walk over to an apple tree with a pair of scissors, and cut an apple from the tree, I will then have an understanding of gravity, as I watch and observe the apple fall to the ground. The wisdom in this example would be to NOT jump off a building without a parachute!

Here is another example, this one is from A.A. Milne and our friends that lived in the Hundred Acre Wood. Rabbit has knowledge that Winnie The Pooh's backside is stuck in his doorway. Rabbit has understanding that help is on the way, and that he really doesn't have much control over the situation. Rabbit then uses his wisdom to make good of the situation while choosing to continue his day without strife. Rabbit wisely moves his life in a positive direction in spite of his circumstances!

Before Gaining Wisdom

fina
After Gaining Wisdom

lly, from the biblical perspective, Jesus was known to speak in parables when He would preach amongst the people. His disciples asked Him why he did that. Jesus gave His answer in **(Matt 13:11-13)** "Because it has been given to you to know the mysteries of the kingdom of heaven, but to them it has not been given. For whoever has, to him more will be given, and he will have abundance; but whoever does not have, even what he has will be taken away from him. Therefore I speak to them in parables, because seeing they do not see, and hearing they do not hear, nor do they understand."

If you are a chosen child of God, then you have been given the ability to know and understand the hidden messages in the Word, through seeing and hearing; once you understand, you are then led to wisdom and God's point of view regarding your life. You want to become one of the "haves" and not one of the "have nots" if you are going to finish your journey and follow your path to your life purpose.

Knowledge, understanding and wisdom are the keys to life. Discover your destiny and create your legacy!

Traveling Through The Gate

Make a list of (5) situations or stories, similar to the apple example, that demonstrate you have learned how Knowledge, Understanding, and Wisdom work together!

Choose (5) scriptures from the Book of Proverbs, and explain how Knowledge and Understanding were used to produce the Wisdom shown.

Victory in Healing

- Illness, Despair, and Poverty Mindsets -

God wants you well, and living in abundance. There is healing power in the mind. You are empowered to heal yourself, but many people don't seem to understand this concept. People are always begging God to heal them or begging God to not let them get "what is going around". If you truly understood the victory in healing, then I think you would choose to change your mental focus regarding sickness and illness, am I right?

You have to claim victory in your life! Don't conform to the world or to the behavioral patterns of others. The Greek word for Victory is nike which means a conquest, triumph, the means of success. So to overcome the world is to live in victory and thus live with triumph and success! Unfortunately, sickness and illness has become a normal way of life for a lot of people. They expect to get sick and they accept it when it happens. This is so disheartening to watch, because the opposite can happen, but you have to claim it first. You have to know who you are and that you have victory in healing!

I don't allow sickness or illness in my life; it's unproductive. My spirit and the Holy Spirit lives in my body, otherwise known as a dwelling, a temple or a tent. Therefore, illness has no place in my body and it's not allowed! With all due respect to my spirit and the Holy Spirit, it is my job to keep everything pure in my body! We are not to grieve the Holy Spirit **(Eph 4:30)**. The same is true for you, but you must believe in healing and take authority over your body. While others are getting sick (because they caused it or allowed it) you tell the sickness to go away - you take authority over the sickness! It helps if you speak this authority out loud - "You do not have permission to enter my body! You come near me, you will die!" I say that to any sickness or illness that tries to come at me! Everything with a name must bow. **(Phil 2:10)**

It is written in **(Exodus 23:25)** "And you shall serve the Lord your God ... I will TAKE sickness away from the mist of thee." The Hebrew word for take is sur which means to turn off, remove or keep away. Turn off or keep away sickness!?! God will turn off sickness on the inside of you! Sickness does not have to be a part of your life. Expect to be well! Expect favor and receive health! I don't allow sickness into my body, because I stand on the Word! If I feel any "symptoms" coming on, I speak out loud that I am healed! I speak TO the illness and tell it that I don't allow it in my body! I tell it to get out, and I heal myself! I have done this time and time again. While I'm surrounded by people who expect to get sick because its "flu season etc.", I REFUSE to GET sick, because I've made it clear, that I don't allow it! No plague shall come near my dwelling! **(Psalm 91)** You too have this power if you stand on the Word of God!

If you feel you are under attack, then resist the devil, and he will flee from you! **(James 4:7)** Always speak THAT out loud as well. I wipe that guy off the bottom of my shoe on a regular basis – that is if he even dares to get that close to me. I am a favored, blessed, and protected child of God, and he is treading on treacherous ground to even get close to me. My heavenly army of angels, spirits and guides will kick him into the next century if he tries to touch a hair on my head! You are THAT protected as well; but you have to believe it and claim it!

You have God's power to heal yourself. Command injury, sickness, illness, despair to leave your life – the minute you feel it coming on! You have God's power at your command. It's already there, right inside of you. Live in God's best and in God's victory! Overcome the world! Stop asking God for what you already have! Get plugged in!

I liken this to the electricity in your home. Its always there, you just have to plug in or flip a switch to activate it. The same is true for God's power that lives on the inside of you. Its always there, but you have to plug in and activate it in your life! **(Ps 91)** says that no plague [sickness] shall come near your dwelling or tent [body]. Speak that out loud! Believe it and receive it! Even God spoke the world into existence! **(Prov 18:21)** says that death and life are in the hand [power] of the tongue. You have to believe and SPEAK TO your situation; THEN, what you speak will come to pass!

God gave YOU supernatural empowerment and authority. In **(Mark 11:23)** it is written that YOU should speak to YOUR mountain [problem]. It does not say to pray to God so that He can remove your problem for you. It says that YOU have authority over YOUR problem! YOU are to speak to your problem in order to remove it or heal it!

There is empowerment in your words! In **(Matt 10)** it is written that YOU are to heal <u>ALL</u> sickness and disease, YOU are to do the healing! God gave YOU authority over your health and wellness!

You have already been given the authority to heal yourself! You are already healed! So many people cry out to God and ask HIM to heal them, but He is not going to do that. He already gave YOU all power and authority over being sick **(Matt 10:8)**. You must speak TO the problem. One of my favorite books is *"The Authority of the Believer"* by Andrew Wommack. I've listed this title in the suggested reading section of this book. There is no need for me to add excerpts from his book here, you can buy it and read it for yourself! I highly recommend all of Andrew's books, especially THIS one. It's a very powerful teaching. Check it out!

Jesus healed you and you received this empowerment to heal long ago. In **(1 Peter 2:24)** it is written that by His wounds you <u>WERE</u> healed! So, stop asking and begging God to heal you! If sickness, illness, despair, depression or any other ailment is present in your life, then this is a wonderful area of study for you to consider while doing your work. God wants you well and living in abundance. He wants you to heal your entire essence; body, soul and spirit!

God truly wants you living in abundance! Poverty mindsets are not God's best. You can't give if you don't have, and we are commanded to love, give to, and serve others. If we are living with a poverty mindset, then we are not able to fulfill this command. I'm not just talking about finances here, I'm talking about loving yourself as well! The words of Jesus are recorded in **(Luke 4:18-19)** "The Spirit of the Lord is upon Me; therefore He anointed Me to preach the gospel to the poor; He has sent Me to heal the brokenhearted, to preach deliverance to captives, and new sight to the blind, to send away crushed ones in deliverance; to preach an acceptable year of the Lord." The word acceptable in the Greek is dektos which means approved, propitious and favorable; a good chance of success. We are to do the same works as Jesus and we are to choose to live in abundance where there is enough for everyone! If you have a poverty mindset or choose to live in poverty, how can you bless other people? If you live paycheck to paycheck, or you are living with just enough to get by, you are living with a poverty mindset. Break free from that way of life! You have been given the spirit of victory and the ability to overcome the world. Get out of your flesh and walk in the spirit, with faith, protection and abundance!

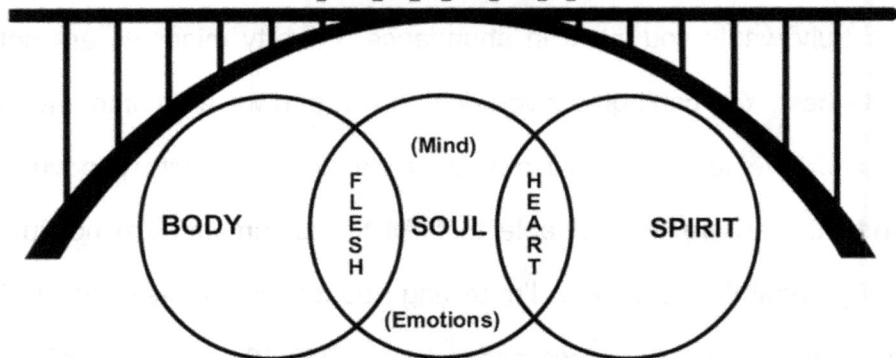

FAITH

BODY | FLESH | SOUL (Mind) (Emotions) | HEART | SPIRIT

In **(1 John 5:4)** it is written "For whatever is born of God overcomes the world; and this is the victory that has overcome the world -- our faith." All faith and belief of protection must be spoken out loud! There is empowerment in your words, and we have been given authority to speak TO the problem. When you speak, you are releasing your faith and authority over the matter! Remember that faith is the bridge between the spiritual and the physical **(Figure 4)**. Speak words in faith! Command any sickness, illness, despair or poverty mindset to GO AWAY! Your words have the empowerment to do so!

Become ONE with Divine Love; the highest form of love! Live your life with this higher frequency, and keep yourself separated from lower frequency lifestyles such as sickness, illness and poverty.

You have been healed! Live in victory over illness, despair and poverty mindsets!

Traveling Through The Gate

List (5) areas of your body that need healing.
List (5) areas of your soul that need healing.
List (5) areas of your spirit that need healing.

Where are you injured or broken? Take time to command healing for each area, utilizing the spiritual power inside of you! You deserve to experience victory and freedom!

Raising Your Vibration

- Renewing Your Mind -

You are commanded to live a changed life through the renewing of your mind **(Romans 12:2)** "Be transformed (changed) by the renewing of your mind. Be not conformed to this age". The Greek word for renew is anakainosis which means to re-establish (a relationship) and resume with change. The Greek word for mind is nous which means intellect and understanding. The Greek word for age is aion which means a period of time that we spend in the world without end forever more. It is also written in **(Eph 4:21-24)** that we are to putt off damaging behaviors of the flesh and put on renewing behaviors of the spirit. "If indeed you have heard Him and have been taught by Him, as the truth is in Jesus: that you put off, concerning your former conduct, the old man which grows corrupt according to the deceitful lusts, and be renewed in the spirit of your mind, and that you put on the new man which was created according to God, in true righteousness and holiness." If you need a refresher regarding these put off / put on scriptures, go back and review them in the chapter entitled *Absolve Yourself From Fear – How To Stop Conforming To The World.* **(Table 1 - p. 77)**

When you renew your mind, you put OFF living in your own strength (low vibrational behaviors) and put ON living in God's strength – perfect divine love (high vibrational behaviors). You should choose to operate and live in the spirit, with God's power, Divine Love, and protection.

When you renew your mind, you stop operating in a low vibrational state of worry and fear and you start operating in the high vibrational state of Divine Love. Fear is a form of punishment and love drives out fear!

It is written in **(James 4:10)** that we are to humble ourselves in order to be exalted. When we act out of humility, we allow ourselves to be lifted up into a higher vibrational state! You will find that your vibrational energy will actually attract similar vibrations. What you think about, comes back to you. When you can't control what is happening, control the way you respond to what is happening, that is where your power is! You have been given a spirit of empowerment; once you renew your mind, you can fight and resist ANYTHING!

In **(Table 2)** you will see a list of behaviors and their corresponding vibrational energies from LOW to HIGH. Become aware of your choices of behaviors and lifestyles. Learn to leave behind LOW vibrational behaviors and work towards living with HIGH vibrational behaviors. Learn to leave behind behaviors of the flesh (LOW) and work towards operating from the heart in the spirit (HIGH). Learn to operate with authority in God's best with God's strength!

(E)motions = Energy in Motion. Energy vibrates at a certain frequency. The Law of Vibration activates the Law of Attraction & through the Law of Deservedness you attract what you send out by the emotions you hold in your body. Change your vibrational frequency and CHANGE YOUR RESULTS! Again, what you think about comes back to you. Energies attract like energies!

Where thoughts go energy flows! The Universe doesn't know the difference between a penny and a Million dollar bill. What ever you believe FOR, you will get more OF! You get what you think about whether it is a positive or negative thought. The Universe is basically a mirror and reflects your own thoughts right back to you. If you worry,

Vibrational Scale of Consciousness

Emotion	Your Vibe	Life Space	Through The Gates - Do The Work	
Awakened	HIGH	HEART	Awakening to Spirit	East
Love / Joy			Love, Faith, Joy & Peace	South
Peace			Love, Faith, Joy & Peace	South
Enthusiasm			Knowledge, Understanding & Wisdom	North
Acceptance			Awakening to Spirit	East
Positivity			Raising Your Vibration	North
Hopefulness			Absolving From Fear	South
Willingness			Self-Control & Balance	West
Desire			Obedience	East
Courage			Releasing Your Power	East
Disconnected			Awakening to Spirit	East
No Identity			Awakening to Spirit	East
Inadequacy			Expecting Miracles	West
Guilt			Actions & Consequences	West
Doubt			Living Outside the Natural	East
Blame			Healing	North
Jealousy			Relating to Others	South
Depression			Healing	North
Anger / Hatred			Knowledge, Understanding & Wisdom	North
Fear	LOW	FLESH	Absolving From Fear	South

Table 2 - Vibrational Scale of Consciousness

you will get more worry. If you focus on abundance then abundance will be yours! You must guard your thoughts and get out of harmful fleshly behaviors and patterns. You must instead focus on thoughts that will activate spiritual behaviors and patterns. The choice is yours to make. Will you choose to live in the flesh or choose to live in the spirit?

When you do the work to renew your mind, you will begin to fill your mind with God's Word. Your mind is like a tank, and when you start filling it with new information, the old will get flushed out. Renewing your mind with the Word of God will leave no room for junk, trash, negativity or other low vibrational behaviors or mindsets. "Therefore we do not lose heart. Even though our outward man is perishing, yet the inward man is being renewed day by day." **(2 Corin 4:16)**

When you choose to operate from the spirit, you choose to operate in a higher vibrational state. It is written in **(Isaiah 40:31)** "and those who wait on the Lord shall renew their strength; they shall mount up with wings like eagles, they shall run and not be weary, they shall walk and not faint."

Raise your vibrational energy by renewing your mind!

Traveling Through The Gate

List (5) situations where you responded from a low vibrational state. Ask yourself why you chose this route? What was your payoff for doing so? Revisit each situation, and reflect on how you could have responded from a higher vibrational state! Remember, whatever vibration you put out, you will get back!

Awakening To Your Life Purpose

- Doing The Work -

Important note: Before beginning your work, make sure that you have completed all of the appropriate *[Traveling Through The Gate]* exercises provided to you at the end of each chapter.

Life challenges and life experiences have placed you along certain paths during your lifetime, in order to help you awaken to your life purpose. Looking through the list of gates and paths which we have discussed **(Table 3)**, try to identify those that heavily resonate with you, and those that you would like to work on. You may choose the paths that have "called to you" while reading this book, and you may also choose the paths that have given you the most difficulty in your life so far.

If you are uncertain where to begin your work, go back and review any of the gates that have left you pondering or yearning for more information.

Doing the work is a process and takes time. Ask God and your angels to help you identify the paths and the gates through which you need

Exploring Your Ascending and Descending Paths As You Travel Through the Gates Awakening to Your Life Purpose		
Direction	The Gate	The Path
The Spiritual Gates Of the East	1	Obedience
	2	Courageously Releasing Your God Given Power
	3	Knowing Who You Are
		Awakening To Spirit
The Emotional Gates Of the South	4	Love, Faith
		Joy, Peace
		Forgiving Self
		Forgiving Others
	5	Goodness, Kindness & Gentleness
		Sympathy / Empathy
	6	No More Fear
The Physical Gates Of the West	7	Servitude
		Gratitude
		Generosity
	8	Self-Control
		Balance
	9	Expecting Miracles
The Mental Gates Of the North	10	Knowledge, Understanding & Wisdom
	11	Living in Victory
		Healing
		Mental Focus
	12	Raising Your Vibration

Table 3 – The Gates and Paths – Doing the Work

to travel in order to awaken to your life purpose and to discover your life plan. It's important that you do the work from your heart space, not from your flesh! Its time to stop existing and start seeking. Its time to stop guessing and start finding. Its time for you to get out of your flesh, and start operating from the heart!

"For I know the thoughts that I think toward you, says the Lord, thoughts of peace and not of evil, to give you a future and a hope." **(Jer 29:11)**

Once you have identified the paths that you would like to work on, try to identify the life challenge or the life experience that put you there. Identify the gate(s) through which you will be traveling to complete your work. Once you are on the right path and traveling through the correct gate(s), God will give you the desires of your heart, then the plans that He has for you will come into full focus as you forge ahead on your journey to finding and serving your life purpose! Don't be surprised if what God shows you turns out to be much different than the result you thought you were looking for. God took me down a path that I never saw coming. It's a path that I now cherish, and one that I can now see was meant for me from the very beginning.

If you have made it this far through *The 12 Gates of Heaven*, I congratulate you for having the courage to face some very difficult personal issues along the way. Doing the work and traveling to find your life purpose, can be very exciting as well as very perplexing and intimidating.

Harness the God given supernatural power that you have found inside of you, and forge ahead in faith, from your heart. I have taken this journey myself, and I can tell you that there IS a light at the end of the tunnel, you have nothing to be afraid of, and the promised land awaits you!

I will meet you when you return home.

Till then...... safe travels....

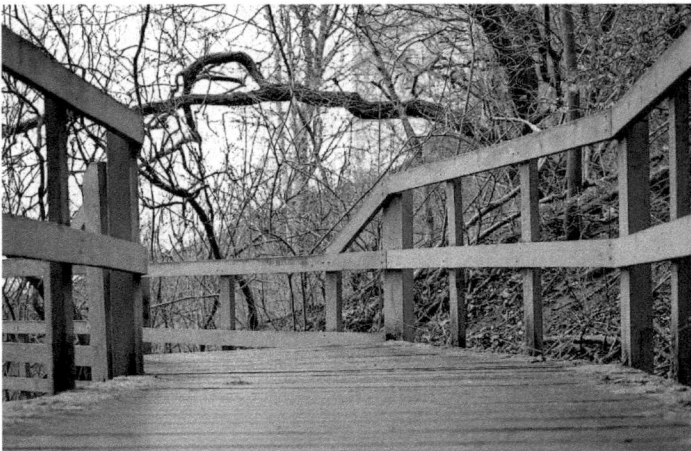

APPENDIX

A Word From the MAIN Gate:
John 14 – 15 – 16

My Love Letter to God:
A Personal Walk Through the Scriptures

Suggested Reading

About the Author

About Freedom Spirit Prison Outreach

A Word From The MAIN Gate:

John 14 – 15 – 16

From the New American Standard Bible - (NASB)

At the conclusion of the Last Super, the night before his crucifixion, Jesus spoke to his disciples. His words are recorded in John 14, 15, & 16 of the bible. You too are one of his disciples, therefore this message is for YOU as well. Pay close attention to what He has to tell you. Read it over several times, and study His message further if you feel called to do so! Seek, and you shall find!

John 14

Jesus Comforts His Disciples (You)

"Do not let your heart be troubled; believe in God, believe also in Me. 2 In My Father's house are many dwelling places; if it were not so, I would have told you; for I go to prepare a place for you. 3 If I go and prepare a place for you, I will come again and receive you to Myself, that where I am, there you may be also. 4 And you know the way where I am going." 5 Thomas said to Him, "Lord, we do not know where You are going, how do we know the way?" 6 Jesus said to him, "I am the way, and the truth, and the life; no one comes to the Father but through Me.

Understanding (Your) Oneness with the Father

7 If you had known Me, you would have known My Father also; from now on you know Him, and have seen Him."

8 Philip said to Him, "Lord, show us the Father, and it is enough for us." 9 Jesus said to him, "Have I been so long with you, and yet you have not come to know Me, Philip? He who has seen Me has seen the Father; how can you say, 'Show us the Father'? 10 Do you not believe that I am in the Father, and the Father is in Me? The words that I say to you I do not speak on My own initiative, but the Father abiding in Me does His works. 11 Believe Me that I am in the Father and the Father is in Me; otherwise believe because of the works themselves. 12 Truly, truly, I say to you, he who believes in Me, the works that I do, he will do also; and greater works than these he will do; because I go to the Father. 13 Whatever you ask in My name,

that will I do, so that the Father may be glorified in the Son. 14 If you ask Me anything in My name, I will do it. 15 If you love Me, you will keep My commandments."

Role of the Holy Spirit - Your Helper - The Spirit of Truth

16 "I will ask the Father, and He will give you another Helper, that He may be with you forever; 17 that is the Spirit of truth, whom the world cannot receive, because it does not see Him or know Him, but you know Him because He abides with you and will be in you."

18 "I will not leave you as orphans; I will come to you. 19 After a little while the world will no longer see Me, but you will see Me; because I live, you will live also. 20 In that day you will know that I am in My Father, and you in Me, and I in you. 21 He who has My commandments and keeps them is the one who loves Me; and he who loves Me will be loved by My Father, and I will love him and will disclose Myself to him." 22 Judas (not Iscariot) said to Him, "Lord, what then has happened that You are going to disclose Yourself to us and not to the world?" 23 Jesus answered and said to him, "If anyone loves Me, he will keep My word; and My Father will love him, and We will come to him and make Our abode with him. 24 He who does not

love Me does not keep My words; and the word which you hear is not Mine, but the Father's who sent Me.

25 "These things I have spoken to you while abiding with you. 26 But the Helper, the Holy Spirit, whom the Father will send in My name, He will teach you all things, and bring to your remembrance all that I said to you. 27 Peace I leave with you; My peace I give to you; not as the world gives do I give to you. Do not let your heart be troubled, nor let it be fearful. 28 You heard that I said to you, 'I go away, and I will come to you.' If you loved Me, you would have rejoiced because I go to the Father, for the Father is greater than I. 29 Now I have told you before it happens, so that when it happens, you may believe. 30 I will not speak much more with you, for the ruler of the world is coming, and he has nothing in Me; 31 but so that the world may know that I love the Father, I do exactly as the Father commanded Me. Get up, let us go from here."

John 15

Jesus Is the Vine - Followers (You) Are Branches Of the Vine That Bear Fruit

"I am the true vine, and My Father is the vinedresser. 2 Every branch in Me that does not bear fruit, He takes away; and every branch that bears fruit, He prunes it so that it may bear more fruit. 3 You are already clean because of the word which I have spoken to you. 4 Abide in Me, and I in you. As the branch cannot bear fruit of itself unless it abides in the vine, so neither can you unless you abide in Me. 5 I am the vine, you are the branches; he who abides in Me and I in him, he bears much fruit, for apart from Me you can do nothing. 6 If anyone does not abide in Me, he is thrown away as a branch and dries up; and they gather them, and cast them into the fire and they are burned. 7 If you abide in Me, and My words abide in you, ask whatever you wish, and it will be done for you. 8 My Father is glorified by this, that you bear much fruit, and so prove to be My disciples. 9 Just as the Father has loved Me, I have also loved you; abide in My love. 10 If you keep My commandments, you will abide in My love; just as I have kept My Father's commandments and abide in His love. 11 These things I have spoken to you so that My joy may be in you, and that your joy may be made full."

Jesus Commands His Disciples (You) To Love One Another
12 "This is My commandment, that you love one another, just as I have loved you. 13 Greater love has no one than this, that one lay

down his life for his friends. 14 You are My friends if you do what I command you. 15 No longer do I call you slaves, for the slave does not know what his master is doing; but I have called you friends, for all things that I have heard from My Father I have made known to you. 16 You did not choose Me but I chose you, and appointed you that you would go and bear fruit, and that your fruit would remain, so that whatever you ask of the Father in My name He may give to you. 17 This I command you, that you love one another."

Disciples' (Your) Relation to the World

18 "If the world hates you, you know that it has hated Me before it hated you. 19 If you were of the world, the world would love its own; but because you are not of the world, but I chose you out of the world, because of this the world hates you.

20 Remember the word that I said to you, 'A slave is not greater than his master.' If they persecuted Me, they will also persecute you; if they kept My word, they will keep yours also. 21 But all these things they will do to you for My name's sake, because they do not know the One who sent Me. 22 If I had not come and spoken to them, they would not have sin, but now they have no excuse for their sin. 23 He

who hates Me hates My Father also. 24 If I had not done among them the works which no one else did, they would not have sin; but now they have both seen and hated Me and My Father as well.

25 But they have done this to fulfill the word that is written in their Law, 'They hated Me without a cause.' 26 When the Helper comes, whom I will send to you from the Father, that is the Spirit of truth who proceeds from the Father, He will testify about Me, 27 and you will testify also, because you have been with Me from the beginning."

John 16

Jesus' Warning

"These things I have spoken to you so that you may be kept from stumbling. 2 They will make you outcasts from the synagogue, but an hour is coming for everyone who kills you to think that he is offering service to God. 3 These things they will do because they have not known the Father or Me. 4 But these things I have spoken to you, so that when their hour comes, you may remember that I told you of them. These things I did not say to you at the beginning, because I was with you."

The Holy Spirit Promised – He Will Disclose (to You) What Is To Come

5 "But now I am going to Him who sent Me; and none of you asks Me, 'Where are You going?' 6 But because I have said these things to you, sorrow has filled your heart. 7 But I tell you the truth, it is to your advantage that I go away; for if I do not go away, the Helper will not come to you; but if I go, I will send Him to you. 8 And He, when He comes, will convict the world concerning sin and righteousness and judgment; 9 concerning sin, because they do not believe in Me; 10 and concerning righteousness, because I go to the Father and you no longer see Me; 11 and concerning judgment, because the ruler of this world has been judged."

12 "I have many more things to say to you, but you cannot bear them now. 13 But when He, the Spirit of truth, comes, He will guide you into all the truth; for He will not speak on His own initiative, but whatever He hears, He will speak; and He will disclose to you what is to come. 14 He will glorify Me, for He will take of Mine and will disclose it to you. 15 All things that the Father has are Mine; therefore I said that He takes of Mine and will disclose it to you."

Jesus' Death and Resurrection Foretold – Your Grief Will Become Joy

16 "A little while, and you will no longer see Me; and again a little while, and you will see Me." 17 Some of His disciples then said to one another, "What is this thing He is telling us, 'A little while, and you will not see Me; and again a little while, and you will see Me'; and, 'because I go to the Father'?" 18 So they were saying, "What is this that He says, 'A little while'? We do not know what He is talking about." 19 Jesus knew that they wished to question Him, and He said to them, "Are you deliberating together about this, that I said, 'A little while, and you will not see Me, and again a little while, and you will see Me'? 20 Truly, truly, I say to you, that you will weep and lament, but the world will rejoice; you will grieve, but your grief will be turned into joy. 21 Whenever a woman is in labor she has pain, because her hour has come; but when she gives birth to the child, she no longer remembers the anguish because of the joy that a child has been born into the world. 22 Therefore you too have grief now; but I will see you again, and your heart will rejoice, and no one will take your joy away from you."

Prayer Promises – Your Father Is With You So That You May Have Peace In The World

23 "In that day you will not question Me about anything. Truly, truly, I say to you, if you ask the Father for anything in My name, He will give it to you. 24 Until now you have asked for nothing in My name; ask and you will receive, so that your joy may be made full."

25 "These things I have spoken to you in figurative language; an hour is coming when I will no longer speak to you in figurative language, but will tell you plainly of the Father. 26 In that day you will ask in My name, and I do not say to you that I will request of the Father on your behalf; 27 for the Father Himself loves you, because you have loved Me and have believed that I came forth from the Father. 28 I came forth from the Father and have come into the world; I am leaving the world again and going to the Father."

29 His disciples said, "Lo, now You are speaking plainly and are not using a figure of speech. 30 Now we know that You know all things, and have no need for anyone to question You; by this we believe that You came from God." 31 Jesus answered them, "Do you now believe? 32 Behold, an hour is coming, and has already come, for

you to be scattered, each to his own home, and to leave Me alone; and yet I am not alone, because the Father is with Me. 33 These things I have spoken to you, so that in Me you may have peace. In the world you have tribulation, but take courage; I have overcome the world."

Θαρσεῖτε ἐγὼ νενίκηκα τὸν κόσμον

Receive the Holy Spirit

As a child of God, your Heavenly Father wants you to have the supernatural power that you need in order for you to use your God given potential and awaken to your life purpose!

When you are ready, just ask, believe and receive! Claim your supernatural power through prayer!

Pray, *"Father, I recognize my need for Your power to live this new life. Please fill me with Your Holy Spirit. By faith, I receive it right now! Thank you for baptizing me with Your supernatural power! Holy Spirit, You are welcome in my life!"*

I'm happy that you took this step to receive supernatural power in your life. Use it wisely; ask God and the Holy Spirit for help as you travel through the gates to find your life purpose. Live a life full of blessings, favor and protection!

My Love Letter To God:

A Personal Walk Through the Scriptures

Many years ago, my bible began to literally fall apart due to the many miles it had traveled with me along my spiritual journey. I decided to gather all of my study notes from this particular bible, so that I could study them anew in the original languages of the Hebrew and Greek. I then purchased the 4 volume set of *The Interlinear Bible* (which you will find in the suggested reading section of this book) and began to further study my notes and the accompanying scriptures by means of the original languages in which they had been written. It was from this new study, which took me months to complete, that my love letter to God evolved. This study enabled me to meditate on the Word in its original languages and speak it right back to God in my letter, furthering my understanding of what had been written. I wanted to share my love letter with you here. Enjoy.

L

God almighty, you have established your covenant with me. You have set your rainbow in the air, and it shall be a sign. Angels run to and fro the heavens, delivering messages and providing protection to me. You have given me the land on which I lie. You are with me, you guard me in every place I go and you bring me to your promised land, never to forsake me.

You have sent an angel which goes before me, to guard me in my way, and to bring me to the place which you have prepared for me. Your name is in him. You are my God and your law is firmly stamped upon my heart. I shall only look to you; you speak with me from the heavens, and you are my source. I have found favor in your eyes Lord and you know me by name. Show me your Glory Lord, I recognize and receive your favor and mercy.

My spiritual eyes are open to seek you Lord and my ears readily listen for your commands. Your angels surround me; although they remain invisible to my carnal eye, I know they are there. It is you, Jehovah my God, that gives me the power to get wealth. Your covenant is established among your people, a special treasure out of all the peoples who are on the face of the earth.

You bless me in the city and bless me in the field. My basket is blessed; I am blessed when I come in, and when I go out. Jehovah, you shall cause my enemies that rise up against me to be stricken before my face. They shall come out against me one way, and flee before me seven ways. Jehovah, you bless my storehouses and all that I set my hand to and you bless me in the land which you gave to me. People will know that I am called by your name, and you shall open to me your good treasure. You have made me the head and not the tail, above and not beneath.

My Lord, you have set before me life and death, blessings and curses. I therefore choose life that I may live, to love you, Jehovah my God, to listen to your voice and to cleave to you. For you are my life and the length of my days. I am strong, and I am brave. I do not fear, as you are with me. You shall never fail me nor forsake me. Every place on which my foot shall tread, you have given it to me. Your book of the law shall not depart from my mouth. I shall meditate on it day and night, so that I shall be on guard to do according to all that is written in it. For then, I will prosper in my ways and I will act wisely. I will not be afraid or discouraged, for it is you, Jehovah God who is with me in all places where I go.

O

God, you are my rock. I will take refuge in you. You are my shield, my strength, my protection and you give me victory in my salvation. You shall save me from violence and I shall be saved from my enemies. You hear my voice, you hear my cry, and you protect me.

You send your angels to me when I am in despair. They encourage me, they pick me up, and empower me to move on in a positive direction. Bless me, my Lord, enlarge my border and keep your hand with me always. Keep me from evil so that it may not grieve me. I rejoice in the Glory of your name, Father. I give thanks to you continuously, remembering the wonders you have done. I will remember your covenant forever and I proclaim your salvation. You are great, Jehovah and you are praised, you are to be feared above all gods. Honor and majesty are before you; strength and gladness are in your place.

Almighty God, I choose to serve you with a perfect heart and with a willing mind, for you search out all hearts and you understand every imagination of thoughts. Blessed are you God, the God of Israel, my Father, for ever and ever. It is written that your eyes run to and fro in all the earth in order to be strong for those who have their heart perfect towards you. I receive that strength and I know that you are with me. I work and I prosper when I seek you with my whole heart.

Psalm 19 is my favorite psalm and it brings me joy whenever I read it. Let the words of my mouth and the meditation of my heart be pleasing in Your sight, O Jehovah, my rock and my Redeemer. Psalm 23 reminds me how near you are and reminds me of the continuous blessings that you rain down upon me. I am forever grateful. You are my light and my salvation, whom shall I fear? You are the strength of my life, of whom shall I be afraid? Teach me your way, Jehovah, and lead me in a level path, because of those who watch me. My hope is in you. I receive your blessings and mercy embraces me because I trust in you.

Your eyes, Jehovah, are on the righteous and your ears are open to my cry. You serve me out of all of my distresses and worries. You give me the desires of my heart. You tell me to be still and know that you are God. You are exalted among the nations and in the earth. Create in me a clean heart, O God, and renew a steadfast spirit within me.

V

Jehovah, you are my rock and my fortress. You continuously protect me and command your angels concerning me. Your angels are mighty in strength, doing your Word and listening to your voice. Psalm 119 showcases the Hebrew aleph-bet and is an expression of praise and celebration for your Word. As it says in Cheth, favor me according to your Word. My help comes from you Lord, the maker of the heavens and the earth. You created me and it is my time to be here. I can't hide from you. Search me, O God and know my heart and know my thoughts. I will praise you with the sound of music; let everything that breathes praise Jehovah!

The book of Proverbs was written to be a book of wisdom. I will trust in you with all of my heart and I will not lean on my own understanding. Your words are life to me because I found them and they are healing to all of my flesh. My ways are before you Lord, and you see everything. I understand that there are 7 things that are detestable to you: a proud look, a lying tongue, hands that shed innocent blood, a heart that plots evil plans, feet hurrying to run to mischief, a false witness who breathes lies, and he who causes strife among brothers.

Proverbs 8 teaches me about knowledge, understanding and wisdom. Wisdom calls and understanding gives her voice. I found you and therefore I found life. I have obtained favor from you, Jehovah. Your Word teaches that if I refresh others, I too will be refreshed. Your Word teaches against pride, as pride goes before destruction. Many purposes are in my heart, but your counsel will stand. In other words, it is laughable to tell YOU what MY plans are. You direct my steps and you measure my heart. Your Word reminds me that as a man thinks in his heart, so is he. Your Word reminds me to live each day to the fullest and to assist or encourage others as iron sharpens iron.

I acknowledge that you are my source, O Lord. I trust in you and receive justice. The fear of man brings a snare, but he trusting Jehovah is set on high. The book of Ecclesiastes explains the purpose of life; noted by wisdom, wine (pleasures), work, wealth and women. Confirmation is given in chapter 12 where the end of life is discussed – when the spirit returns to God who gave it. You promise in your Word that I will prosper along with the city where you have placed me. You know the life purpose that you have for me, a purpose of peace and not evil, to give me a future and a hope.

E

It is written in your Word, that I shall not live by bread alone, but by every word going out of the mouth of God. It is written that I shall not tempt the Lord my God. It is written that I shall worship the Lord my God and I shall serve Him only. I am the salt of the earth, and I am truly blessed. I am a pure and divine being of light. By following your commands, I am able to walk on water just like Peter did.

Your Word says that if I have, more will be given and I will abound, but from him who does not have, even that which he has will be taken from him. My heart is lush soil on which I plant your seed. I desire to grow that seed to produce visible fruit for the Kingdom and for those around me. I will not set aside your commandments in order to keep my own traditions, for that makes the Word of God of no effect. Traditions of men are just that, traditions. And, I will not let your Word get in the way of what my flesh desires. Only you put the desires on my heart. I will follow your way. All things are possible to me, because I believe in you and your Word. If I have anything against anyone, I will forgive it, so that you, my Father in Heaven will forgive my sins.

It is written that I should give, and good measure will be given to me pressed down and shaken together, and running over. For the same measure which I measure, it will be measured back to me. Your Word says that my name is written in heaven and that you have given me the authority to tread on snakes and scorpions, and on all the power of the Enemy, and nothing shall hurt me, at all.

It is written that you God, are a spirit and that all who worship you must worship you in spirit and truth. It is also written that no one is able to come to Jesus unless you, the Father, draws him.

If I continue in your Word, I am your disciple, and I will know the truth and the truth will set me free! Jesus came that I may have life and that I may have it abundantly. I am a killer sheep!

I cherish the scriptures of John 14-15-16, as this written Word captures what Jesus said to his disciples before he died. I am a disciple and therefore, these words were spoken for me and TO me as well.

The Holy Spirit has come upon me and I have received power along with the gifts of the Holy Spirit, including speaking in tongues. Just like Stephen, full of faith and power, I will do wonders and great miracles among the people. And, just like you did for Paul, you will guide my path, even changing its course if it's necessary for my higher good.

The Spirit of life in Christ Jesus has set me free from the law of sin and of death. I have the mind of the Spirit which is life and peace. Christ lives in me as does the Spirit of the One having raised him from the dead. As I pray, the Spirit himself pleads my case with groanings that cannot be uttered. I have been called according to purpose. You foreknew me and you predestined me to be conformed to the image of your Son. Since I was predestined, I was also called, justified and glorified. No one can come against me and nothing shall separate me from the love of Christ.

You have raised me up, so that I might show forth your power in me and so that your name may be publicized in all the earth. I am saved, for I have confessed the Lord Jesus with my mouth and have believed in my heart that you raised Him from the dead. The riches, the wisdom and the knowledge of you, God is deep. Because of You and through You, and to You ARE all things!

I present my body to you Lord, a living sacrifice, holy, pleasing to you which is your reasonable service. I am not conformed to this age, but I am transformed by the renewing of my mind in order to prove what is your good and pleasing, perfect will. I am obedient to you in my faith, Lord. I accept the mysteries that have been revealed to me through scripture. Your Word is truth and it is firmly planted in my heart. I speak the wisdom of you, God in a mystery, having been hidden, which you predestined before the ages for my glory. Through the gifts of the Spirit, I have been given wisdom, a word of knowledge, faith, gifts of healing, workings of powers, prophecy, discerning of spirits, and interpretations of languages. Faith, hope and love remains, but the greatest of these is love.

Death has been swallowed up in victory through my Lord, Jesus Christ. I will be firm, unmovable, abounding in the work of the Lord always, knowing that my labor is not without fruit in the Lord. I will maintain that balance between the physical and the spiritual until my last day, when I shall return home.

I am a new creation in Christ. When I am at home in my body, I am away from home from you Lord. I walk by faith, not by sight, I am fully assured then and am pleased to go, away from home out of the body, and to come home to you Lord. I am reconciled to you God; through Jesus, I have become the righteousness of you in Him. God, you are able to make all grace abound towards me, that in everything, always having all self sufficiency, I might abound to every good work.

Christ has redeemed me from the curse of the law, having become a curse for me. I have received the promise of the Spirit through faith. Through that faith, I have become a daughter of Christ Jesus. If I am lead by the Spirit, and not by my flesh, I am not under the law. The fruit of the Spirit is love, joy, peace, longsuffering, kindness, goodness, faith, meekness, self control – against such things there is not a law. I live in the Spirit, and therefore I walk in the Spirit.

I have been given a spirit of wisdom and revelation in the knowledge of you. The eyes of my mind have been enlightened for me to know what is the hope of your calling. I understand the surpassing greatness of power towards me, the same power that you worked in Christ when raising him from the dead. It was by grace that I was saved, through faith, and not of myself. It is the gift of you, God. Not of works, that I should boast, for I am your workmanship, created in Christ Jesus unto good works, which you prepared before me that I should walk in them.

I do not desire to grieve the Holy Spirit; for it was through Him that I have been sealed to the day of redemption. It is my desire to be kind to all, forgiving others as you have forgiven me in Christ. I want to stand up out of the dead ones that surround me, and allow Christ to shine upon me. I will give thanks at all times for all things in the name of my Lord Jesus Christ and to you, God, my Father. I stand firm, fully dressed with the armor of God, so that I may continue to resist in this evil day – My loins are girded with the truth, and I wear the breast plate of righteousness. My feet are shod with the preparation of the gospel of peace and I hold the shield of faith. I wear the helmet of salvation and the sword of the Spirit, which is the Word of God, and I continue to pray in the Spirit on all occasions.

Christ will be magnified through my body, whether through life or death. And, just like Paul mentioned, I have a desire to depart and be with Christ, which is far better, but I will remain in the body until such time my purpose has been served. As Christ demonstrated, I will be humble and obedient until I depart. I choose to forget the things which are behind me and I choose to press forward to all things before me, especially the prize of the high calling of you in Christ Jesus. My work is from the soul, as to the Lord and not to men. I know that from the Lord I will receive the reward of the inheritance. I choose to let your peace rule in my heart, and I am gracious and thankful for all that you have done for me. I will rejoice always. God, your peace fully sanctifies me. My whole spirit, soul and body is kept blameless at the coming of our Lord Jesus Christ. He who calls me is faithful.

You God offer me everything and my hope is in you. You are my source! You did not give me a spirit of fearfulness, but instead you gave me power, love, and self control. I shall endure with you and be faithful. My goal is to be gentle to all with an apt for teaching, in hope that the truth may reach those who need to learn it. I acknowledge that very scripture is God-breathed and profitable for teaching, for reproof, for correction and for instruction in righteousness. It's through the Word that I am fully furnished for every good work.

When I depart from this earth, I will have fought the good fight, I will have finished the course and will have kept the faith. I look forward to that day, when I can return home to be with you.

My purpose in life is to share my faith with others and to refresh others through the joy and encouragement that I have in your son, Jesus Christ. I acknowledge that faith is the substance of things hoped for, the evidence of things not being seen. I will patiently run the race that has been set before me, looking to the author and finisher of my faith, Jesus Christ.

You Lord are my helper, and I will not be afraid, what shall man do to me? I am content with what I have, you protect me and provide for me. You are my source for all things. You have revealed your son, Jesus Christ to me, whom I love and whom I have not seen, but I exalt him with unspeakable joy. I have been glorified because I believe in him, yet I have not seen him. You God, are no respecter of persons and I am Holy because you are Holy. You have purified my soul in the obedience of truth through the Spirit.

Peter and Paul both proclaimed that our bodies are tabernacles or tents. Peter spoke the truth about what he had seen; that he was an eyewitness to the teachings and miracles of your son, Jesus Christ. It is through this written Word that I too believe the same things, even though I have not seen them. Every word of scripture did not come into being by its own interpretation, for the Word was not born by the will of man, but having been born along by the Holy Spirit, holy men of God spoke. Thank you for your Word, it is the truth, and the lamp which lights my path.

I can overcome anything, because you are in me, and I hear you. You have taught me how to discern spirits; any spirit which does not confess that Jesus Christ has come in the flesh, is not from you. You have taught me how to love. You are love, and I am from you and you first loved me. You have taught me that because you love me, I am also to love my brother and fellow man. I am to love as I have been loved and I am to forgive as I have been forgiven.

The Spirit is the one witnessing to me, because the Spirit is the truth. For it is written: there are three bearing witnesses in Heaven: the Father, the Word, and the Holy Spirit; and these three are one. It is written that I have everlasting life, because I believe in the name of the Son of God. If I ask anything according to your will, you hear me.

And, since I know that you hear me, whatever I ask, I know that I have what I have asked from you.

I build myself up by my holy faith, praying in the Holy Spirit while keeping myself in your love. I eagerly await my eternal life. You are the Alpha and the Omega, the Beginning and the Ending. You freely give to me the fountain of the water of life. I will overcome and I will inherit all things.

I love you!

- Judy

Suggested Reading

Beckwith, Michael B. 2012. *Life Visioning: A Transformative Process for Activating Your Unique Gifts and Highest Potential*. Sounds True Inc.

Braden, Gregg. 2008. *The Divine Matrix: Bridging Time, Space, Miracles, and Belief*. Hay House, Inc.

Broger, John C. 1991. *Self-Confrontation: A Manual for In-Depth Biblical Discipleship*. Biblical Counseling Foundation.

Byrne, Rhonda. 2006, *The Secret*. Atria Books/Beyond Words.

Green, Jay P. 2005. *The Interlinear Bible including the Hebrew-Aramaic Old Testament and the Greek-English New Testament (4 Volume Set)*. Hendrickson Publishers.

Linn, Denise. 2015. *Kindling the Native Spirit*. Hay House Inc.

Schwartz, Robert. 2009. *Your Soul's Plan: Discovering the Real Meaning of the Life You Planned Before You Were Born*. Frog Books.

Schwartz, Robert. 2012. *Your Soul's Gift: The Healing Power of the Life You Planned Before You Were Born.* Whispering Winds Press

Sirovina, Hrvoje. 2019. *Redeeming your Bloodline: Foundations for Breaking Generational Curses from the Courts of Heaven*. Destiny Image Publishers, Inc.

Smart, Ralph. 2013. *Feel Alive*. London. Infinite Waters Publishing, Inc.

Wilkinson, Bruce. 2000. *The Prayer of Jabez: Breaking Through to the Blessed Life.* Multnomah Publishers, Inc.

Wommack, Andrew. 2008. *The New You & the Holy Spirit.* Andrew Wommack Ministries Inc.

Wommack, Andrew. 2009. *The Believer's Authority: What You Didn't Learn In Church.* Harrison House Publishers.

Wommack, Andrew. 2010. *Spirit, Soul & Body.* Harrison House Publishers.

Wommack, Andrew. 2011. *Sharper than a Two-Edged Sword: A Summary of Sixteen Powerful Messages that have Changed the Lives of Thousands.* Harrison House Publishers.

Wommack, Andrew. 2012. *Self-Centeredness; The Source of All Grief.* Harrison House Publishers.

Wommack, Andrew. 2019. *The Power of Imagination: Unlocking Your Ability to Receive from God.* Harrison House Publishers.

About the Author

Judy Faass was born and raised in Atlanta, Georgia and now makes her home in the beautiful mountains of Colorado, where she has lived for two decades. When she isn't spending her time working or serving others, she spends her time hiking, biking and exploring nature in the vast wilderness, otherwise known as her backyard of spiritual freedom. Judy is also the founder and director of Freedom Spirit Prison Outreach, a non profit corporation that advocates for and comes along side those who are incarcerated and their families. The Outreach offers hope, encouragement, growth and transformation to those on the inside, while assisting them with re-entry preparations.

About Freedom Spirit Prison Outreach
With your help, we unlock and develop potential from the inside out!

The Prison Outreach was founded and began reaching out to incarcerated individuals during the summer of 2019. As the outreach continued to reach and correspond with multiple offenders throughout the US, a common thread began to unfold and the truth began to reveal itself. Most incarcerated individuals are set up to fail. They are kept within the confines of a negative, hostile and controlled environment, stripped of their natural abilities and personalities while being provoked and harassed by people who are supposedly there to help them.

Families who try to support and help their loved ones on the inside, eventually become overwhelmed and numb to the possibility that they can do anything further to help. When they try, they are often given the run-around, given false hope, or even ignored. Family members eventually withdraw, leaving their incarcerated loved one to fend for themselves. This isn't an act of hatred or abandonment, its an act of hopelessness. They just can't cope anymore.

Knowing these facts, the Outreach has developed a program that allows outside advocates, to come along side the incarcerated and their families in an effort to turn things around; to turn the negative into a positive, to turn the darkness into a visible light. We listen, provide exercises and self – help resources to those on the inside so that they can see that change and transformation is in fact possible, that they can change their ways and grow – in a positive and successful direction. Their past does not have to define them!

As an outreach, we also come along side the wrongfully convicted as they struggle to make sense of being falsely accused, struggle to make sense of being betrayed by a co-defendant who took a plea deal and left them holding the bag, or struggle to make sense of being lied to and coerced into a false confession by a corrupt police force.

Today's prison sentences, handed down by our judicial system, tend to run consecutively, in order to "protect the public", leaving young offenders, often 19-21 years of age, with staggering long sentences of 30 to 65 years; some are given life sentences. For many of these youthful offenders, this was their first crime, or their first time behind bars. Now, they are left to grow up in prison while spending their crucial developmental years in a hostile environment. Our 20's are the defining decade of our adulthood. 80% of life's most defining moments take place before age 35. How does incarcerating our youth for decades, help them to grow, mature and respect life with any kind of hope?

The incarcerated have names, they are not merely numbers in a system. The Outreach works with those who demonstrate that they are interested in working hard to create change. We will not enable, or coddle, or give them false hope. We believe that everyone deserves to have the chance to live their life with purpose, irregardless of their current circumstances. Therefore, we offer our services and we come along side of the incarcerated and their families to make that happen!

Fundraising for Freedom Spirit Prison Outreach is accomplished through individual and business donations and the sale of inspirational greeting cards which are sold to the "outside" to send to the "inside". Some of the greeting cards utilize art and messages which have been designed, created and donated by those who are incarcerated.

Contact Us to Join the Outreach

or to

Make a Donation:

FreedomSpiritPrisonOutreach@Gmail.com

(202) 417-6554

www.Facebook.com/PrisonAdvocacy

www.FreedomSpiritBooks.com

GET THE WORKBOOK!

THE 12 GATES OF HEAVEN

DISCOVER YOUR GOD GIVEN POTENTIAL
AND
AWAKEN TO YOUR LIFE PURPOSE

WORKBOOK

JUDY FAASS

ISBN: 978-1-71-511678-1 (Paperback)

This companion WORKBOOK is written in an easy to follow format for individual or group study. The WORKBOOK is designed to help you explore your life journey and discover your life purpose while deeply assessing your own life, life direction, and changes that you desire to make in your day to day existence. The WORKBOOK will assist you as you "do the work" to discover the life you were meant to live!

Available at

amazon

blurb

and other global booksellers and retailers